Engineering Materials: Properties, Processing, and Applications

Cory Eric

Copyright © [2023]

Title: Engineering Materials: Properties, Processing, and Applications
Author's: Cory Eric

All rights reserved. No part of this publication may be reproduced, stored in a retrieval system, or transmitted in any form or by any means, electronic, mechanical, photocopying, recording, or otherwise, without the prior written permission of the publisher or author, except in the case of brief quotations embodied in critical reviews and certain other non-commercial uses permitted by copyright law.

This book was printed and published by [Publisher's: **Cory Eric**] in [2023]

ISBN

TABLE OF CONTENT

Chapter 1: Introduction to Engineering Materials   10

Overview of Materials Science and Engineering

Importance of Engineering Materials

Classification of Engineering Materials

Structure of Engineering Materials

Properties of Engineering Materials

Processing of Engineering Materials

Applications of Engineering Materials

Chapter 2: Atomic Structure and Bonding   28

Atomic Structure

Types of Bonding

Crystal Structures

Defects in Crystals

Chapter 3: Mechanical Properties of Materials   36

Stress and Strain

Elastic Deformation

Plastic Deformation

Strengthening Mechanisms

Fracture and Failure

Fatigue and Creep

Chapter 4: Thermal Properties of Materials   49

Heat Transfer

Thermal Expansion

Thermal Conductivity

Thermal Insulation

Chapter 5: Electrical and Magnetic Properties of Materials — 57

Electrical Conductivity

Insulators and Semiconductors

Dielectric Materials

Magnetic Materials

Chapter 6: Phase Diagrams and Phase Transformations — 65

Phase Diagrams

Phase Transformations

Diffusion

Chapter 7: Materials Processing Techniques   71

Casting

Forming

Machining

Welding

Heat Treatment

Surface Treatment

Chapter 8: Metals and Alloys   84

Ferrous Metals and Alloys

Non-ferrous Metals and Alloys

Metal Matrix Composites

Shape Memory Alloys

Chapter 9: Polymers and Composites   93

Polymers: Structure and Properties

Polymer Processing

Composite Materials: Types and Properties

Fiber Reinforced Composites

Polymer Matrix Composites

Chapter 10: Ceramics and Glasses   103

Ceramic Materials: Structure and Properties

Traditional Ceramics

Advanced Ceramics

Glass: Structure and Properties

Glass-Ceramics

Chapter 11: Materials Selection and Design 114

Material Selection Criteria

Design Constraints and Considerations

Material Designation Systems

Case Studies: Material Selection in Engineering Applications

Chapter 12: Applications of Engineering Materials 123

Structural Materials

Electronic and Optoelectronic Materials

Biomaterials

Environmental and Energy Materials

Materials for Transportation

Materials for Aerospace Applications

Chapter 13: Future Trends in Materials Science and Engineering   135

Emerging Materials

Nanomaterials and Nanotechnology

Sustainable Materials

Materials for 3D Printing

Materials for Advanced Electronics

Chapter 14: Conclusion and Summary   145

Recap of Key Concepts

Future Prospects in Materials Science and Engineering

Final Thoughts

Chapter 1: Introduction to Engineering Materials

Overview of Materials Science and Engineering

Materials Science and Engineering is a multidisciplinary field that combines principles from physics, chemistry, and engineering to study the structure, properties, processing, and applications of materials. It plays a crucial role in the development of new materials and technologies that have revolutionized various industries, including aerospace, automotive, electronics, and healthcare.

In this subchapter, we will provide an introduction to the field of Materials Science and Engineering, outlining its importance and relevance to engineers. We will explore the fundamental concepts, methodologies, and applications that engineers in this niche should be familiar with.

Firstly, we will delve into the basic principles of materials science, discussing the atomic structure of materials and how it affects their properties. This includes topics such as crystal structures, grain boundaries, defects, and phases. Understanding these fundamental concepts is essential for engineers to design and select materials that meet specific performance requirements.

Next, we will explore the various properties of materials, including mechanical, thermal, electrical, and magnetic properties. Engineers need to have a comprehensive understanding of how materials behave under different conditions and how to manipulate these properties through processing techniques. We will discuss the relationships between structure, properties, and performance, emphasizing the importance of materials characterization and testing methods.

The subchapter will also cover different classes of materials, such as metals, ceramics, polymers, and composites. We will discuss their unique properties, processing methods, and applications in engineering. Furthermore, we will highlight the importance of material selection, considering factors such as cost, availability, environmental impact, and sustainability.

In addition to the fundamentals, we will explore the various processing techniques used in materials engineering, such as casting, forming, welding, and additive manufacturing. Engineers must understand these processes to optimize material properties and achieve desired performance characteristics.

Lastly, we will discuss the applications of materials science and engineering in various industries. From lightweight and high-strength materials for aerospace applications to biocompatible materials for medical devices, we will showcase the impact of materials science on technological advancements.

Overall, this subchapter aims to provide engineers in the niche of Materials Science and Engineering with a solid foundation in the field. By understanding the principles, properties, processing, and applications of materials, engineers will be equipped to make informed decisions and develop innovative solutions to engineering challenges.

Importance of Engineering Materials

Introduction:

In the field of engineering, materials play a crucial role in the design, development, and application of various products and structures. Understanding the importance of engineering materials is fundamental for engineers, especially those specializing in materials science and engineering. This subchapter aims to emphasize the significance of engineering materials and their impact on the overall success of engineering projects.

1. Materials Selection:

Engineering materials serve as the building blocks for any project. From bridges and buildings to microchips and medical implants, the selection of appropriate materials determines the performance, durability, and safety of the final product. Engineers must consider factors such as mechanical properties, thermal conductivity, corrosion resistance, and electrical conductivity when choosing materials for specific applications. The right material selection can optimize performance, reduce costs, and enhance the overall efficiency of engineering projects.

2. Material Processing:

Understanding the processing techniques for engineering materials is crucial for engineers to achieve desired properties and performance. Materials processing involves various techniques such as casting, forging, welding, and heat treatment. Each process imparts specific characteristics to the material, enabling engineers to tailor it according to the project requirements. By understanding the processing techniques, engineers can optimize material properties and achieve desired product performance.

3. Material Performance:

The performance of engineering materials directly impacts the functionality, reliability, and safety of the final product. For example, in aerospace engineering, lightweight materials with high strength-to-weight ratios are essential to ensure fuel efficiency and structural integrity. Similarly, in the medical field, biocompatible materials are crucial for the success of implants and prosthetics. Engineers must have a deep understanding of material performance to ensure the longevity and reliability of their designs.

4. Material Innovation:

Advancements in engineering materials drive technological progress in various industries. New materials with improved properties and performance are constantly being developed, enabling engineers to push the boundaries of what is possible. From nanomaterials to composite materials, continuous innovation in engineering materials opens up new avenues for engineering solutions, leading to more efficient and sustainable designs.

Conclusion:

The importance of engineering materials cannot be overstated. Materials selection, processing techniques, material performance, and material innovation all play a critical role in the success of engineering projects. Engineers specializing in materials science and engineering must continually enhance their knowledge and stay updated with the latest advancements in materials technology. By doing so, they can harness the power of engineering materials to create innovative and sustainable solutions that shape the future of various industries.

Classification of Engineering Materials

In the vast field of engineering, materials play a crucial role in determining the success and efficiency of any project. The selection of appropriate materials is essential for achieving the desired performance and functionality of engineering structures and components. To understand and make informed decisions about materials, engineers must have a comprehensive knowledge of their classification.

Classification of engineering materials is based on various aspects such as their composition, structure, properties, and applications. This classification system helps engineers identify the right materials for specific tasks, ensuring the desired outcomes are achieved. In this subchapter, we will explore the different classifications of engineering materials and their significance in materials science and engineering.

One commonly used classification is based on the chemical composition of materials. This classification includes metals, ceramics, polymers, and composites. Metals are known for their high strength, ductility, and electrical conductivity, making them ideal for structural applications. Ceramics, on the other hand, possess excellent thermal and chemical resistance, making them suitable for high-temperature applications. Polymers, including plastics and elastomers, offer lightweight and flexible properties, making them ideal for a wide range of applications. Composites combine the unique properties of different materials to create advanced materials with enhanced performance.

Another classification criterion is based on the crystalline structure of materials. This classification includes crystalline and amorphous materials. Crystalline materials have a highly ordered atomic arrangement, resulting in well-defined properties and predictable behavior. Amorphous materials lack a regular atomic structure and exhibit unique properties such as transparency and high resistance to fracture.

Additionally, materials can be classified based on their mechanical, thermal, electrical, and magnetic properties. This classification helps engineers select materials that meet specific requirements for a particular application. For example, materials with high strength and toughness are suitable for structural components, while materials with excellent thermal conductivity are ideal for heat transfer applications.

Understanding the classification of engineering materials is crucial for engineers working in materials science and engineering. By having a thorough knowledge of the different material classes and their properties, engineers can make informed decisions regarding material selection, processing techniques, and design considerations. This knowledge enables engineers to optimize the performance, reliability, and cost-effectiveness of engineering structures and components.

In conclusion, the classification of engineering materials is a fundamental aspect of materials science and engineering. By categorizing materials based on their composition, structure, and properties, engineers can effectively select the most suitable materials for different applications. This understanding facilitates the development of innovative solutions, ensuring the successful implementation of engineering projects. As engineers, it is imperative to continuously update our knowledge of material classifications to stay at the forefront of advancements in materials science and engineering.

Structure of Engineering Materials

The structure of engineering materials is a fundamental aspect of materials science and engineering. It refers to the arrangement and organization of atoms, molecules, and grains within a material. Understanding the structure of materials is crucial for engineers as it directly influences their mechanical, thermal, electrical, and chemical properties. In this subchapter, we will delve into the fascinating world of material structures and explore their significance in various engineering applications.

At the atomic level, materials can have different crystal structures, such as cubic, hexagonal, or tetragonal. These structures determine how atoms are arranged and bonded together, which greatly impacts the material's properties. Engineers must have a thorough understanding of crystal structures to design materials with desired characteristics.

Furthermore, materials can exhibit different types of bonding, including metallic, covalent, ionic, and van der Waals forces. Each bonding type contributes to the material's overall strength, ductility, and electrical conductivity. Engineers must consider these bonding characteristics when selecting materials for specific applications, such as designing lightweight aircraft components or high-strength alloys for automotive parts.

Moreover, the grain structure of a material is another critical aspect of its overall structure. Grain boundaries are the interfaces between individual crystal grains within a material. The size, orientation, and distribution of these grains can significantly affect the material's mechanical properties, such as strength, toughness, and fatigue resistance. Engineers often manipulate the grain structure through heat treatments and alloying to improve the overall performance of materials.

In addition to crystal structures and grain boundaries, engineers must also understand the concept of defects in materials. Defects, such as vacancies, dislocations, and impurities, can impact the material's mechanical, electrical, and thermal properties. By understanding and controlling these defects, engineers can enhance the material's performance and reliability.

Lastly, this subchapter will also discuss the characterization techniques used to analyze and determine the structure of engineering materials. Techniques like X-ray diffraction, scanning electron microscopy, and transmission electron microscopy provide valuable insights into the atomic and microstructural features of materials. Engineers must be familiar with these techniques to evaluate and optimize the structural properties of materials.

In conclusion, the structure of engineering materials plays a vital role in determining their properties and performance. This subchapter provides engineers with a comprehensive understanding of the various aspects of material structures, including crystal structures, bonding types, grain boundaries, defects, and characterization techniques. By mastering these concepts, engineers can effectively select, design, and process materials for a wide range of applications, ensuring optimal performance and reliability in their engineering endeavors.

Properties of Engineering Materials

Introduction:
The study of engineering materials is a vital component of the field of materials science and engineering. Understanding the properties of different materials is crucial for engineers to select the right materials for specific applications. This subchapter aims to provide a comprehensive overview of the properties of engineering materials, enabling engineers to make informed decisions during the design and manufacturing processes.

Mechanical Properties:
One of the primary considerations for engineers is the mechanical properties of materials. These properties include strength, stiffness, hardness, toughness, and ductility. Strength refers to a material's ability to withstand external forces without deformation or failure. Stiffness determines a material's resistance to deformation under load, while hardness relates to its resistance to indentation or scratching. Toughness measures a material's ability to absorb energy before fracturing, and ductility refers to its ability to deform under tensile stress without breaking.

Thermal Properties:
The thermal properties of materials play a critical role in engineering applications. These properties include thermal conductivity, specific heat capacity, and coefficient of thermal expansion. Thermal conductivity indicates how well a material conducts heat, while specific heat capacity measures its ability to store heat. The coefficient of thermal expansion determines how much a material expands or contracts with changes in temperature. Engineers must consider these

properties when designing systems that involve heat transfer or temperature variations.

Electrical Properties:

In many engineering applications, electrical properties must be taken into account. These properties include electrical conductivity, resistivity, dielectric strength, and permittivity. Electrical conductivity refers to a material's ability to conduct electric current, while resistivity measures its opposition to the flow of electric current. Dielectric strength indicates a material's ability to withstand voltage without electrical breakdown, and permittivity determines its ability to store electrical energy in an electric field.

Chemical Properties:

Engineers also need to consider the chemical properties of materials to ensure their suitability for specific environments or applications. These properties include corrosion resistance, chemical reactivity, and compatibility with other substances. Corrosion resistance refers to a material's ability to resist degradation when exposed to corrosive substances. Chemical reactivity determines how a material interacts with other chemicals, and compatibility refers to its ability to coexist with other materials without adverse effects.

Conclusion:

A deep understanding of the properties of engineering materials is essential for engineers in the field of materials science and engineering. Mechanical, thermal, electrical, and chemical properties all play significant roles in material selection and design. By considering these properties, engineers can ensure that materials are chosen appropriately for specific applications, leading to efficient and successful engineering projects.

Processing of Engineering Materials

Introduction:
In the field of engineering, materials play a crucial role in the design and fabrication of various structures and components. Understanding the processing of engineering materials is essential for engineers to ensure optimal performance, reliability, and safety. This subchapter delves into the various techniques and processes involved in the processing of engineering materials, providing engineers with valuable insights into the world of materials science and engineering.

1. Material Selection:
The processing of engineering materials begins with the careful selection of appropriate materials for a specific application. Engineers must consider factors such as mechanical properties, chemical compatibility, thermal stability, and cost-effectiveness when choosing materials for their designs. This section provides an overview of the principles and criteria involved in material selection, helping engineers make informed decisions.

2. Forming Processes:
Forming processes involve shaping materials into desired forms using various techniques such as casting, forging, rolling, extrusion, and sheet metal forming. Engineers need to understand the principles and limitations of these processes to achieve the desired shape, size, and dimensional accuracy. This section explores each forming process in detail, highlighting their advantages, drawbacks, and applications.

3. Joining Techniques:
Joining techniques are crucial for assembling different components

and materials in engineering applications. Welding, brazing, soldering, adhesive bonding, and mechanical fastening are some of the commonly used joining techniques. This section discusses the principles, procedures, and challenges associated with each joining technique, enabling engineers to select the most appropriate method for their specific requirements.

4. Heat Treatment:
Heat treatment processes involve controlled heating and cooling of materials to alter their microstructure and improve their mechanical properties. Engineers must have a deep understanding of heat treatment techniques such as annealing, quenching, tempering, and case hardening to optimize the performance and durability of engineering materials. This section covers the fundamentals of heat treatment, including the effects of temperature, time, and cooling rate on material properties.

5. Surface Engineering:
Surface engineering techniques are employed to modify the surface properties of materials, enhancing their wear resistance, corrosion resistance, and aesthetic appeal. Surface treatments such as plating, coating, surface modification, and surface finishing are explored in this section, along with their applications in engineering.

Conclusion:
The processing of engineering materials is a multifaceted domain that requires a comprehensive understanding of materials science and engineering principles. This subchapter serves as a valuable resource for engineers in the field of materials science and engineering, equipping them with the knowledge and skills necessary to select,

process, and optimize materials for diverse applications. By delving into the intricacies of material selection, forming processes, joining techniques, heat treatment, and surface engineering, engineers can unlock the full potential of engineering materials and contribute to the advancement of various industries.

Applications of Engineering Materials

Engineering materials play a crucial role in the field of Materials Science and Engineering. These materials are carefully designed, selected, and processed to meet the specific requirements of various applications. This subchapter explores the wide range of applications of engineering materials and highlights their significance in various engineering disciplines.

One of the primary applications of engineering materials is in the construction industry. Materials such as steel, concrete, and aluminum alloys are extensively used in the construction of buildings, bridges, and infrastructure projects. Steel, known for its high strength and durability, is commonly used in the construction of skyscrapers and bridges. Concrete, on the other hand, offers excellent compressive strength and is utilized in the construction of foundations and structures that require resistance to harsh environmental conditions. Aluminum alloys are lightweight and corrosion-resistant, making them ideal for applications in the aerospace industry and automobile manufacturing.

Another essential application area for engineering materials is in the field of transportation. The automotive sector heavily relies on materials such as high-strength steels, aluminum alloys, and composites to enhance fuel efficiency, reduce weight, and improve safety. These materials are used in the manufacturing of automobile bodies, engine components, and structural parts. Additionally, materials like carbon fiber composites are extensively employed in the aerospace industry due to their high strength-to-weight ratio, contributing to the development of lighter and more fuel-efficient aircraft.

Engineering materials also find applications in the electronics and electrical industry. Materials such as semiconductors, ceramics, and polymers are essential for the production of electronic devices, circuit boards, and electrical insulators. Semiconductors are crucial for the functioning of transistors and integrated circuits, forming the backbone of modern electronics. Ceramics are used in the production of insulators and capacitors, while polymers are utilized in the manufacturing of flexible circuits and electrical connectors.

Moreover, engineering materials are extensively employed in the medical field. Biocompatible materials such as titanium alloys and bioactive glasses are widely used in the production of medical implants, prosthetics, and dental applications. These materials possess excellent mechanical properties and compatibility with the human body, ensuring optimal performance and patient safety.

In conclusion, engineering materials have diverse applications across various engineering disciplines. From construction and transportation to electronics and healthcare, these materials enable the development of innovative technologies and solutions. Understanding the properties, processing techniques, and applications of engineering materials is essential for engineers in the field of Materials Science and Engineering to design and create reliable and efficient products and structures.

Chapter 2: Atomic Structure and Bonding

Atomic Structure

In the field of materials science and engineering, a thorough understanding of atomic structure is crucial. The study of atomic structure provides engineers with the necessary foundation to comprehend the behavior and properties of different materials. This subchapter aims to delve into the intricacies of atomic structure, exploring its components, organization, and significance in engineering applications.

At its core, an atom is the basic building block of matter. Engineers must understand the fundamental components of an atom, which include protons, neutrons, and electrons. Protons possess a positive charge, neutrons are electrically neutral, and electrons carry a negative charge. These subatomic particles are arranged in specific energy levels or shells around the nucleus.

The organization of electrons in these energy levels plays a significant role in determining an atom's properties. Engineers should have a firm grasp on the concepts of valence electrons, electron configurations, and the periodic table. Valence electrons are the outermost electrons of an atom and are responsible for the bonding behavior of atoms. This knowledge is vital for engineers when designing and selecting materials for specific applications.

Furthermore, engineers must comprehend the concept of isotopes and their impact on material properties. Isotopes are atoms of the same element that have different numbers of neutrons. This variation in neutron count can influence the stability and behavior of materials, affecting their mechanical, thermal, and electrical properties.

Understanding atomic structure also involves the study of crystal structures and their impact on materials. Engineers must recognize the different types of crystal structures, such as cubic, tetragonal, and hexagonal, and how they influence material properties like strength, ductility, and conductivity. This knowledge enables engineers to select appropriate materials for specific applications based on desired properties.

In conclusion, a comprehensive understanding of atomic structure is vital for engineers in the field of materials science and engineering. By grasping the components, organization, and significance of atoms, engineers can make informed decisions about material selection, design, and processing techniques. This knowledge forms the basis for developing innovative materials and optimizing their properties for a wide range of engineering applications.

Types of Bonding

Bonding is a fundamental concept in materials science and engineering that plays a significant role in determining the properties and behavior of different materials. Understanding the types of bonding is crucial for engineers working in the field of materials science and engineering, as it allows them to select the most suitable materials for various applications.

There are three primary types of bonding: metallic bonding, ionic bonding, and covalent bonding. Each type of bonding results from the interaction of atoms or ions and has unique characteristics.

Metallic bonding occurs in metals and is characterized by the sharing of electrons among a lattice of positively charged metal ions. This type of bonding gives metals their unique properties, such as high electrical and thermal conductivity, malleability, and ductility. Engineers often utilize metallic bonding in applications where these properties are desirable, such as electrical wiring, construction materials, and automotive components.

Ionic bonding occurs when there is a transfer of electrons between atoms, resulting in the formation of positive and negative ions. This type of bonding is typically observed in compounds composed of metals and nonmetals. Ionic bonds are relatively strong and lead to the formation of crystalline structures. Engineers frequently employ materials with ionic bonding in applications such as ceramics, batteries, and electronic devices.

Covalent bonding involves the sharing of electrons between atoms, resulting in the formation of strong bonds. This type of bonding is commonly found in nonmetallic elements and compounds. Covalent bonds contribute to the stability and strength of materials, making them suitable for applications where high strength and resistance to deformation are required. Engineers often utilize materials with covalent bonding in industries such as aerospace, automotive, and construction.

In addition to these primary types of bonding, secondary bonding, also known as van der Waals forces, exists between atoms or molecules. Although weaker than primary bonds, secondary bonding is essential for certain materials' properties, such as adhesion and friction. Understanding the balance between primary and secondary bonds is crucial for engineers when designing materials for specific applications.

In conclusion, understanding the types of bonding is vital for engineers in the field of materials science and engineering. By comprehending the characteristics and properties of metallic, ionic, and covalent bonding, engineers can select the most appropriate materials for various applications. Additionally, considering the role of secondary bonding allows for the optimization of material properties and performance.

Crystal Structures

In the fascinating world of materials science and engineering, crystal structures play a fundamental role in understanding the properties and behavior of various materials. A crystal structure refers to the unique arrangement of atoms, ions, or molecules within a crystal lattice, which gives rise to its distinct physical and chemical properties.

Understanding crystal structures is crucial for engineers working in the field of materials science and engineering, as it provides insights into the mechanical, electrical, thermal, and optical properties of materials. By manipulating and controlling the crystal structure, engineers can tailor the properties of materials to meet specific requirements for various applications.

One of the key aspects of crystal structures is the concept of unit cells. A unit cell is the smallest repeating unit within the crystal lattice that represents the entire crystal structure. Engineers use unit cells to describe the symmetry, arrangement, and packing of atoms or ions in a crystal lattice. There are several types of unit cells, such as the simple cubic, body-centered cubic, and face-centered cubic, each having its own unique arrangement of atoms.

Crystal structures can be categorized into different classes based on their symmetry. These classes include cubic, tetragonal, orthorhombic, monoclinic, triclinic, and hexagonal. Each class exhibits a specific arrangement of atoms or ions, resulting in distinct properties. For example, materials with a cubic crystal structure, such as metals like aluminum and copper, tend to have high ductility and conductivity due to their close-packed arrangement of atoms.

Engineers can utilize knowledge of crystal structures to design materials with enhanced properties. By alloying different elements or introducing defects, they can manipulate the crystal structure to improve strength, hardness, corrosion resistance, or other desired properties. For instance, adding small amounts of carbon to iron can transform its crystal structure from a body-centered cubic to a face-centered cubic arrangement, resulting in the formation of harder and stronger steel.

In summary, crystal structures are the foundation of materials science and engineering. Through the study and manipulation of crystal structures, engineers can unlock the hidden potential of materials and create innovative solutions for various applications. This understanding of crystal structures allows engineers to push the boundaries of material performance and develop new materials with tailored properties, ultimately advancing technology and improving our everyday lives.

Defects in Crystals

In the study of materials science and engineering, understanding the defects present in crystals is of utmost importance. Crystals are the building blocks of most materials and possess a highly ordered arrangement of atoms or molecules. However, in reality, perfect crystals are rare to come by. Defects in crystals can occur during the formation process, as a result of external factors, or even due to the inherent nature of the material. These defects can significantly influence the properties, processing, and applications of engineering materials.

There are three main types of defects in crystals: point defects, line defects, and planar defects. Point defects are the simplest type and include vacancies, interstitials, and impurities. Vacancies are vacant lattice sites where an atom or ion is missing, resulting in an imbalance of atomic forces. Interstitials, on the other hand, are atoms or ions that occupy spaces between the normal lattice sites, leading to local lattice distortions. Impurities are foreign atoms or ions that occupy lattice sites, which often alter the material's properties.

Line defects, also known as dislocations, are one-dimensional defects that occur when there is a mismatch in the arrangement of atoms along a line in the crystal lattice. These dislocations can significantly affect the mechanical properties of materials, such as strength, ductility, and hardness. They can also facilitate plastic deformation, allowing the material to undergo permanent shape changes without fracturing.

Planar defects are two-dimensional defects that occur at the boundaries of crystalline regions. Grain boundaries are the most common type of planar defect, arising from the meeting of two or more crystals with different orientations. Grain boundaries can affect the mechanical, electrical, and thermal properties of materials. Other planar defects include stacking faults and twin boundaries, which can influence material behavior at the atomic level.

Understanding the defects in crystals is crucial for engineers working in the field of materials science and engineering. By characterizing and analyzing these defects, engineers can design and develop materials with improved performance and tailored properties. Defects can be intentionally introduced to enhance specific characteristics of materials or eliminated to achieve higher purity and reliability.

In summary, defects in crystals play a crucial role in determining the properties and behavior of engineering materials. Point defects, line defects, and planar defects can significantly influence material properties, processing, and applications. Engineers in the field of materials science and engineering must have a thorough understanding of these defects to manipulate and control material behavior for various technological advancements.

Chapter 3: Mechanical Properties of Materials

Stress and Strain

In the realm of materials science and engineering, understanding the concepts of stress and strain is crucial for designing and analyzing the behavior of various engineering materials. Stress and strain are fundamental mechanical properties that determine how materials respond to external forces and loads. By comprehending the relationship between stress and strain, engineers can develop structures and components that are safe, reliable, and durable.

Stress is defined as the internal force per unit area within a material when subjected to an external load. It is the measure of how much force is applied to a certain area, and it can be expressed mathematically as stress = force/area. Stress can manifest in different forms, such as tensile (pulling apart), compressive (squeezing together), shear (sliding forces), and torsional (twisting). Engineers need to consider the type and magnitude of stress when designing materials to ensure they can withstand the applied loads without failure.

On the other hand, strain refers to the deformation or change in shape experienced by a material when subjected to stress. It is a measure of how much a material is stretched or compressed and can be expressed mathematically as strain = change in length/original length. Strain can be elastic, meaning the material returns to its original shape after the stress is removed, or it can be plastic, indicating permanent deformation. Understanding the relationship between stress and strain is critical for predicting how materials will behave under different loading conditions.

The stress-strain curve is a graphical representation of the relationship between stress and strain. It provides valuable information about a material's mechanical properties, including its strength, stiffness, and ductility. The curve typically consists of three distinct regions: elastic deformation, plastic deformation, and fracture. Engineers analyze this curve to determine the material's yield strength, ultimate tensile strength, and elongation, which are essential parameters for designing structures and selecting appropriate materials.

Moreover, stress concentration is an important phenomenon engineers must consider. It occurs when the stress distribution within a material becomes uneven, leading to areas of high stress concentration. These regions are more susceptible to failure and can cause catastrophic consequences. Engineers employ various techniques, such as adding fillets, chamfers, or reinforcement, to minimize stress concentration and enhance the overall structural integrity.

In conclusion, stress and strain are fundamental concepts in materials science and engineering. By understanding the relationship between stress and strain, engineers can predict and control the behavior of materials under different loading conditions. This knowledge is crucial for designing safe and efficient structures, ensuring the reliability and durability of engineering materials.

Elastic Deformation

In the field of materials science and engineering, the concept of elastic deformation plays a crucial role in understanding the behavior of various materials under different conditions. Elastic deformation refers to the reversible change in shape or size of a material when a force is applied to it, followed by the removal of that force. This subchapter aims to provide engineers with a comprehensive understanding of elastic deformation and its significance in engineering applications.

When a material is subjected to a force within its elastic limit, it undergoes elastic deformation, which means it can return to its original shape and size after the force is removed. This property is essential in numerous engineering applications as it allows materials to withstand external loads without permanent damage. Engineers need to accurately predict and control elastic deformation to ensure the structural integrity and longevity of their designs.

The subchapter will delve into the fundamental concepts and theories that govern elastic deformation, including Hooke's Law. Engineers will learn about stress and strain, which are key parameters used to quantify the magnitude of elastic deformation. The relationship between stress and strain is described by the modulus of elasticity, a material property that varies depending on the type of material.

Furthermore, the subchapter will discuss various factors that influence elastic deformation, such as temperature, time, and the microstructure of materials. Engineers will gain insights into how these factors affect the elastic behavior of different materials, allowing them to make informed decisions when selecting materials for specific engineering applications.

Real-life examples and case studies will be presented to illustrate the practical implications of elastic deformation. These examples will showcase how engineers have successfully utilized elastic deformation to design structures that can withstand external forces, such as bridges, buildings, and aerospace components.

In conclusion, understanding elastic deformation is essential for engineers in the field of materials science and engineering. This subchapter will equip them with the knowledge and tools necessary to accurately predict and control elastic deformation in their designs. By comprehending the behavior of materials under elastic deformation, engineers can ensure the reliability and safety of their structures, contributing to the advancement of the field as a whole.

Plastic Deformation

In the field of materials science and engineering, understanding the concept of plastic deformation is crucial for engineers working with various materials. Plastic deformation refers to the permanent change in the shape or size of a material due to an applied external force. Unlike elastic deformation, which is reversible, plastic deformation causes a material to undergo permanent structural changes.

When a material is subjected to external forces, its atoms or molecules start to move and rearrange themselves. In crystalline materials, plastic deformation occurs through the movement of dislocations – line defects within the crystal lattice. Dislocations allow atoms to shift from one position to another, resulting in plastic flow and deformation.

The ability of a material to resist plastic deformation is referred to as its strength. Different materials exhibit varying levels of strength, which determines their ability to withstand external forces without permanent deformation. The strength of a material is influenced by factors such as its crystal structure, grain size, and impurity content.

Plastic deformation can occur via several mechanisms, including slip, twinning, and grain boundary sliding. Slip is the most common mechanism and involves the movement of dislocations through crystal planes. Twinning, on the other hand, occurs when a portion of the crystal lattice mirrors another portion, resulting in a change in shape. Grain boundary sliding happens when grains in a polycrystalline material slide past each other.

Engineering materials are often designed to possess certain properties that allow them to withstand plastic deformation under specific conditions. For example, in structural applications where high strength is required, materials such as steel or titanium alloys are preferred. These materials have a high yield strength, which means they can withstand significant external forces before undergoing plastic deformation.

Understanding plastic deformation is essential for engineers involved in material selection, processing, and design. By considering a material's mechanical properties and its capacity to withstand plastic deformation, engineers can make informed decisions when choosing the appropriate materials for a particular application. Additionally, engineers can use various techniques, such as heat treatments and alloying, to enhance a material's resistance to plastic deformation.

In conclusion, plastic deformation plays a fundamental role in materials science and engineering. It describes the permanent change in shape or size of a material due to external forces. Engineers must consider a material's strength and its ability to resist plastic deformation when selecting materials for specific applications. By understanding the mechanisms of plastic deformation and employing appropriate techniques, engineers can design materials that can withstand external forces and perform optimally in various engineering applications.

Strengthening Mechanisms

In the field of materials science and engineering, understanding the different mechanisms that enhance the strength and durability of materials is of utmost importance. Strengthening mechanisms play a vital role in determining the performance and reliability of various engineering components. This subchapter aims to provide engineers with a comprehensive understanding of the different ways in which materials can be strengthened to meet the demands of modern applications.

1. Introduction to Strengthening Mechanisms: This section provides an overview of the importance of strengthening mechanisms in materials science and engineering. It introduces the concept of strength and the need to enhance it to withstand external forces and loads. It highlights the significance of selecting appropriate strengthening methods for specific applications.

2. Solid Solution Strengthening: Solid solution strengthening refers to the process of adding alloying elements to a base material to improve its strength. This section explores the mechanisms behind solid solution strengthening, such as atomic size and lattice strain effects. It delves into the role of interstitial and substitutional alloying elements, along with their impact on dislocation movement and grain boundaries.

3. Precipitation Strengthening: Precipitation strengthening involves the formation of fine particles within a material matrix to impede dislocation movement. This section discusses the various precipitation mechanisms, including

nucleation, growth, and coarsening. It also explores the effects of precipitation on grain boundaries and dislocation interactions, emphasizing the importance of heat treatment in optimizing precipitation strengthening.

4. Grain Boundary Strengthening: Grain boundaries play a crucial role in determining the mechanical properties of materials. This section explores the different mechanisms employed to strengthen grain boundaries, such as grain refinement and segregation. It discusses the impact of grain boundary strengthening on deformation behavior, crack propagation, and corrosion resistance.

5. Dislocation Strengthening: Dislocations are line defects in crystal structures that significantly influence the mechanical properties of materials. This section examines the various dislocation strengthening mechanisms, including work hardening, solid-solution hardening, and strain hardening. It highlights the importance of dislocation interactions and obstacles in improving material strength.

6. Other Strengthening Mechanisms: This section discusses additional strengthening mechanisms, including fiber reinforcement, phase transformations, and texture strengthening. It explores the applications of these mechanisms in specific materials, such as composites, shape memory alloys, and textured materials.

7. Summary and Conclusion: The subchapter concludes by summarizing the key points discussed

throughout the chapter. It emphasizes the importance of selecting the appropriate strengthening mechanisms based on the specific requirements of engineering applications. It also encourages engineers to stay updated with advancements in materials science and engineering to leverage new and innovative strengthening techniques.

In conclusion, understanding and applying the various strengthening mechanisms is essential for engineers in the field of materials science and engineering. This subchapter provides a comprehensive overview of the different mechanisms involved in strengthening materials, enabling engineers to make informed decisions in selecting suitable methods to enhance the performance and reliability of their designs.

Fracture and Failure

In the field of materials science and engineering, understanding the behavior of materials under stress is crucial for designing safe and reliable structures. Fracture and failure are two phenomena that engineers encounter frequently, and they play a vital role in determining the mechanical integrity of a material.

Fracture refers to the separation of a material into two or more pieces due to the application of stress. It can occur in various forms, such as ductile fracture or brittle fracture, depending on the material's ability to deform plastically. Ductile materials, like most metals, exhibit significant plastic deformation before fracture, while brittle materials, such as ceramics, fail without any noticeable plastic deformation.

One of the most important concepts in fracture mechanics is the stress concentration factor, which describes the amplification of stress around a geometric irregularity or flaw in a material. Engineers must carefully consider the presence of stress concentrators, such as cracks, notches, or holes, as they significantly reduce the strength and durability of a structure. The study of fracture mechanics allows engineers to predict the growth and propagation of cracks, enabling them to design materials and structures that can withstand the applied loads without catastrophic failure.

Failure, on the other hand, refers to the inability of a material or structure to perform its intended function. Failure can occur due to a variety of reasons, including excessive deformation, fatigue, corrosion, or a combination of factors. Engineers must analyze the potential failure modes and take preventive measures to ensure the safety and reliability of their designs.

To understand fracture and failure, engineers rely on various testing methods, such as tensile tests, impact tests, and fatigue tests. These tests provide valuable information about a material's mechanical properties, including its strength, toughness, and resistance to fracture. By carefully analyzing the test results, engineers can make informed decisions about material selection, processing methods, and design considerations.

In summary, fracture and failure are critical aspects of materials science and engineering. By studying the behavior of materials under stress, engineers can design structures that can withstand the applied loads without catastrophic failure. Understanding fracture mechanics and failure modes enables engineers to enhance the safety, reliability, and performance of materials and structures, contributing to advancements in various industries and ensuring a sustainable future.

Fatigue and Creep

Fatigue and Creep: Understanding the Challenges in Engineering Materials

As engineers in the field of Materials Science and Engineering, it is crucial to have a comprehensive understanding of the behavior of materials under different conditions. Two significant challenges that engineers encounter when designing and working with materials are fatigue and creep. In this subchapter, we will delve into the intricacies of fatigue and creep, exploring their causes, effects, and potential mitigation strategies.

Fatigue is the progressive and localized structural damage that occurs when a material is subjected to cyclic loading. This phenomenon can lead to sudden and catastrophic failures, even in materials that appear to be structurally sound. Engineers must be able to predict and prevent fatigue failure to ensure the reliability and safety of various components and structures. This subchapter will provide a detailed examination of the factors contributing to fatigue, including stress levels, cyclic loading frequency, and material properties. We will also explore methods such as stress-life and strain-life approaches to fatigue analysis, as well as the significance of fatigue limit and endurance limit in materials selection and design.

Creep, on the other hand, refers to the time-dependent deformation that occurs under a constant load or stress. This gradual deformation can compromise the structural integrity of materials, particularly those exposed to high temperatures or prolonged periods of stress. Understanding the mechanisms behind creep and its impact on materials is crucial for engineers working in fields such as aerospace, power generation, and manufacturing. This subchapter will delve into the various types of creep, such as primary, secondary, and tertiary, and discuss critical parameters influencing creep behavior, such as temperature, stress level, and material microstructure. Additionally, we will explore techniques to measure and predict creep deformation, including the use of creep curves and Larson-Miller parameter.

To effectively manage fatigue and creep, engineers must employ suitable material selection, design optimization, and maintenance strategies. This subchapter will highlight the importance of materials testing and characterization, as well as the utilization of advanced modeling and simulation techniques, in predicting and preventing fatigue and creep failures. Furthermore, we will discuss the significance of fatigue and creep life assessment and the development of design guidelines to enhance the durability and performance of materials.

In conclusion, the understanding of fatigue and creep phenomena is paramount for engineers in the field of Materials Science and Engineering. By delving into the causes, effects, and mitigation strategies of fatigue and creep, this subchapter aims to equip engineers with the knowledge necessary to design and work with materials that can withstand the challenges imposed by cyclic loading and time-dependent deformation.

Chapter 4: Thermal Properties of Materials

Heat Transfer

Heat transfer is a fundamental concept in the field of materials science and engineering, playing a crucial role in the selection, design, and processing of engineering materials. Understanding the mechanisms of heat transfer is essential for engineers to effectively manage thermal energy to ensure the optimal performance and reliability of materials and systems.

In this subchapter, we will explore the principles of heat transfer and its various modes: conduction, convection, and radiation. Conduction refers to the transfer of heat through a solid medium, where energy is transmitted through atomic or molecular interactions. Engineers must consider the thermal conductivity of materials when selecting them for specific applications, as it determines how efficiently heat can be transferred through the material.

Convection, on the other hand, involves the transfer of heat through a fluid medium, such as a gas or liquid. This mode of heat transfer relies on the movement of the fluid particles, either through natural convection (caused by density differences due to temperature variations) or forced convection (due to external factors like fans or pumps). Engineers must consider the fluid properties, such as viscosity and thermal conductivity, as well as the flow characteristics when designing heat exchangers, cooling systems, or HVAC systems.

Radiation is the third mode of heat transfer, which does not require a medium for energy transfer. Instead, it relies on electromagnetic waves, such as infrared radiation, to transfer heat energy. Engineers must understand the principles of radiative heat transfer, including emissivity, absorptivity, and reflectivity, to design efficient thermal insulation materials or heat transfer systems that utilize radiation.

Furthermore, engineers need to be aware of the laws governing heat transfer, such as Fourier's law for conduction, Newton's law of cooling for convection, and Stefan-Boltzmann's law for radiation. These laws provide mathematical relationships that enable engineers to calculate heat transfer rates, temperature distributions, and design parameters for various applications.

In conclusion, heat transfer is a critical aspect of materials science and engineering, with profound implications for the performance, design, and processing of engineering materials. By understanding the principles and modes of heat transfer, engineers can make informed decisions in material selection, system design, and thermal management to ensure the efficient and reliable functioning of materials and systems in diverse applications.

Thermal Expansion

Thermal expansion is a fundamental concept in the field of materials science and engineering. It refers to the tendency of materials to expand or contract in response to changes in temperature. Understanding thermal expansion is crucial for engineers as it directly affects the design, performance, and reliability of various engineering materials and structures.

When a material is heated, its atoms or molecules vibrate more energetically, leading to an increase in their average separation distance. This increase in spacing results in the expansion of the material. Conversely, when a material is cooled, the atoms or molecules lose energy and their average separation distance decreases, causing the material to contract.

The magnitude of thermal expansion is different for different materials and is typically quantified by the coefficient of thermal expansion (CTE). CTE is defined as the fractional change in length or volume per degree Celsius or Kelvin temperature change. It is an important property that engineers consider when selecting materials for applications where temperature variations are expected.

Materials with a high CTE are more prone to significant expansion and contraction, while those with a low CTE exhibit minimal dimensional changes. For example, metals generally have higher CTE values compared to ceramics and polymers. This is why metal structures such as bridges and railways require expansion joints to accommodate the thermal expansion and prevent damage.

Thermal expansion can have both positive and negative implications in engineering applications. On one hand, it can be utilized to advantage, such as in the design of bimetallic strips used in thermostats. These strips consist of two different materials bonded together, each with different thermal expansion coefficients. When heated, the strip bends due to the differential expansion, allowing for precise temperature control.

On the other hand, thermal expansion can also be a challenge. For instance, in electronic devices, the mismatch in CTE between different materials can lead to thermal stress and failure. To mitigate this, engineers employ techniques like thermal management systems, using materials with similar CTEs, or employing compliant interconnects that allow for a degree of movement without causing damage.

In summary, thermal expansion is a critical phenomenon that engineers must consider in materials selection, structural design, and thermal management. By understanding the behavior of materials under varying temperatures, engineers can develop robust and reliable systems that can withstand the challenges posed by thermal expansion and contraction.

Thermal Conductivity

In the field of materials science and engineering, understanding the concept of thermal conductivity is crucial. Thermal conductivity refers to the ability of a material to conduct heat. Engineers need to have a strong grasp of this property as it plays a significant role in the design and development of various applications and systems.

Thermal conductivity is a fundamental property that determines how efficiently heat can be transferred through a material. It is defined as the amount of heat that is conducted through a unit area in a unit time when there is a temperature gradient across the material. The unit of measurement for thermal conductivity is watts per meter-kelvin (W/mK).

The knowledge of thermal conductivity is applied in a wide range of industries and engineering disciplines. For instance, in the aerospace industry, understanding thermal conductivity is essential for the development of heat shields and thermal protection systems to ensure the safety of the spacecraft and astronauts during re-entry. Similarly, in the field of electronics, thermal conductivity is crucial for the design of heat sinks and thermal management systems to prevent electronic components from overheating.

Different materials exhibit different thermal conductivities. Metals generally have high thermal conductivity, making them excellent conductors of heat. This is why metal alloys like copper and aluminum are often used in heat exchangers and cooling systems. On the other hand, insulators such as ceramics and polymers have low thermal conductivity, making them suitable for applications where heat transfer needs to be minimized, such as in thermal insulation materials.

Engineers must consider thermal conductivity when selecting materials for specific applications. The ability of a material to efficiently transfer heat can impact the performance, efficiency, and durability of a system. By choosing materials with the appropriate thermal conductivity, engineers can optimize the design of various devices, enhance energy efficiency, and ensure the reliability of their products.

In conclusion, thermal conductivity is a critical property in the field of materials science and engineering. It influences the design and performance of numerous applications and systems across various industries. Engineers must have a thorough understanding of thermal conductivity to select the right materials and develop efficient and reliable solutions.

Thermal Insulation

Thermal insulation is a crucial aspect of materials science and engineering, playing a vital role in various applications across different industries. It is the process of reducing heat transfer between objects or spaces, preventing the loss or gain of heat energy. This subchapter explores the principles, materials, and techniques employed in thermal insulation, highlighting their significance in engineering applications.

Understanding the principles behind thermal insulation is fundamental to harnessing its benefits. Heat transfer occurs through three mechanisms: conduction, convection, and radiation. Conduction is the transfer of heat through direct contact between materials, while convection involves the movement of heat through a fluid medium. Radiation, on the other hand, is the emission of electromagnetic waves, including infrared radiation, which carries heat energy. Effective thermal insulation aims to minimize these heat transfer mechanisms, enhancing the energy efficiency of systems and structures.

A wide range of materials are utilized for thermal insulation, each possessing specific properties suited for particular applications. Common insulation materials include mineral wool, cellulose, fiberglass, and polystyrene foam. These materials exhibit low thermal conductivity, preventing heat transfer and maintaining the desired temperature within a system. Additionally, they often possess other desirable characteristics such as fire resistance, durability, and environmental sustainability.

To achieve optimal thermal insulation, engineers employ various techniques and strategies. One widely adopted approach is the use of insulating materials in building envelopes, including walls, roofs, and floors. These materials help regulate indoor temperatures, reducing the dependence on mechanical heating and cooling systems. Another technique is the incorporation of thermal insulation in industrial equipment, such as pipelines, furnaces, and refrigeration systems. This not only enhances energy efficiency but also improves operational performance and safety.

Engineers involved in materials science and engineering must possess an in-depth understanding of thermal insulation. They must consider factors such as thermal conductivity, thickness, and environmental impact when selecting and designing insulation systems. Moreover, they should stay updated on emerging technologies and advancements in insulation materials to optimize energy efficiency and sustainability in their projects.

In conclusion, thermal insulation is a critical aspect of materials science and engineering, enabling energy efficiency, comfort, and safety in various applications. With the right selection of materials and techniques, engineers can effectively minimize heat transfer, ensuring optimal performance and longevity of systems and structures. Continuous research and innovation in thermal insulation are essential to address emerging challenges and to develop more sustainable and efficient solutions in the field of engineering.

Chapter 5: Electrical and Magnetic Properties of Materials

Electrical Conductivity

In the field of Materials Science and Engineering, understanding the concept of electrical conductivity is of utmost importance. Electrical conductivity refers to a material's ability to conduct electric current. It is a fundamental property that plays a critical role in various engineering applications, from designing electrical circuits to developing advanced electronic devices.

The ability of a material to conduct electricity is dependent on the movement of charged particles, specifically electrons. In conductive materials, such as metals, the outermost electrons of atoms are loosely bound and can move freely. These mobile electrons, also known as conduction electrons, can carry electric charge from one point to another. As a result, metals exhibit high electrical conductivity.

The electrical conductivity of a material is quantified by a physical property called electrical resistivity (or its inverse, electrical conductivity). Electrical resistivity is a measure of a material's opposition to the flow of electric current. It is typically denoted by the Greek letter rho (ρ) and is expressed in ohm-meters ($\Omega \cdot m$).

Different materials exhibit varying levels of electrical conductivity. Metals, such as copper and aluminum, possess high electrical conductivity due to their abundance of free electrons. These materials are widely used in electrical wiring and power transmission due to their ability to efficiently conduct electricity with minimal losses.

In contrast, insulating materials, such as ceramics and plastics, have significantly lower electrical conductivity. These materials have tightly bound electrons, restricting their movement and making them poor conductors of electricity. Insulators are commonly used to prevent the flow of electric current and ensure electrical safety in various applications.

Semiconductors, as the name suggests, exhibit an intermediate level of electrical conductivity between conductors and insulators. They possess a limited number of mobile electrons, which can be controlled by external factors such as temperature or impurities. Semiconductors play a crucial role in modern electronics, serving as the foundation for devices like transistors, diodes, and integrated circuits.

Understanding the electrical conductivity of materials is essential for engineers in designing and optimizing electrical systems and devices. By selecting the appropriate materials with the desired electrical properties, engineers can ensure the efficient and reliable performance of electrical components, circuits, and systems.

In conclusion, electrical conductivity is a fundamental property of materials that determines their ability to conduct electric current. It plays a crucial role in various engineering applications, from power transmission to the development of advanced electronic devices. By understanding the electrical conductivity of different materials, engineers can make informed decisions in selecting the appropriate materials to meet specific design requirements.

Insulators and Semiconductors

In the fascinating field of materials science and engineering, understanding the properties and applications of different materials is crucial for engineers. Among the vast array of materials available, insulators and semiconductors play a pivotal role in various industries and technologies. In this subchapter, we will delve into the world of insulators and semiconductors, exploring their unique characteristics and highlighting their significance in engineering applications.

Insulators, also known as dielectrics, are materials that impede the flow of electric current. They possess high electrical resistivity, making them ideal for preventing the leakage of electricity. Insulators are commonly used in electrical wiring, circuit boards, and insulation materials for electrical devices. Their ability to resist the flow of electrons ensures the safe and efficient functioning of electrical systems. Examples of insulating materials include ceramics, glass, rubber, and certain plastics.

On the other hand, semiconductors are materials that have electrical conductivity between that of insulators and conductors. They exhibit unique properties that allow them to be used in electronic devices and integrated circuits. Silicon and germanium, among others, are widely used semiconductors in the electronics industry. Through the process of doping, impurities are intentionally added to semiconductors to alter their electrical properties and create desired functionalities. This process enables the development of transistors, diodes, and other components crucial for modern technology.

The importance of insulators and semiconductors cannot be overstated in various engineering applications. Insulators play a critical role in ensuring the safety and reliability of electrical systems by preventing short circuits and electrical leakage. Semiconductors, on the other hand, are the backbone of the electronics industry, enabling the development of advanced devices and technologies that have revolutionized our lives.

Engineers specializing in materials science and engineering need to have a deep understanding of the properties and applications of insulators and semiconductors. This knowledge allows them to make informed decisions when selecting materials for specific applications. By understanding the electrical properties, thermal conductivity, and other relevant characteristics of insulators and semiconductors, engineers can design and develop innovative solutions that meet the ever-evolving demands of various industries.

In conclusion, insulators and semiconductors are essential materials in engineering, particularly in the fields of materials science and engineering. Insulators ensure safe and efficient electrical systems, while semiconductors form the foundation of modern electronics. A comprehensive understanding of these materials empowers engineers to make informed choices and develop cutting-edge technologies that continue to shape our world.

Dielectric Materials

Dielectric materials play a crucial role in various fields of engineering, particularly in materials science and engineering. These materials are known for their unique ability to store and release electrical energy, making them essential components in applications such as capacitors, insulators, and energy storage devices. Understanding the properties, processing, and applications of dielectric materials is of utmost importance for engineers working in these fields.

Properties of Dielectric Materials:

Dielectric materials are characterized by their ability to store electrical energy in an electric field. Unlike conductive materials, dielectrics do not allow the flow of electrical current easily. This property is due to their high resistivity, which prevents the movement of electrons. Dielectrics also possess a high dielectric constant, a measure of their ability to store electrical energy. This property is crucial in applications where efficient energy storage is required.

Processing of Dielectric Materials:

Dielectric materials can be processed using various techniques, depending on the specific application requirements. One common method is the deposition of thin films on substrates, which enables the fabrication of miniaturized electronic devices. Other techniques include sintering, polymerization, and sol-gel processes, which allow for the production of dielectric materials with tailored properties.

Applications of Dielectric Materials:

Dielectric materials find extensive use in numerous engineering applications. In the field of capacitors, dielectrics are used to store electrical energy and provide power supply stabilization. Insulators made from dielectric materials are used to prevent the flow of electricity in high-voltage applications, ensuring safety and efficient energy transmission. Dielectric materials are also used in energy storage devices such as batteries and supercapacitors, where their ability to store electrical energy is harnessed.

In the electronics industry, dielectric materials are used in the fabrication of integrated circuits, transistors, and memory devices. They enable the miniaturization of electronic components, leading to more compact and efficient electronic devices. Dielectric materials are also essential in the telecommunications industry, where they are used for the insulation of transmission lines and the production of high-performance antennas.

In conclusion, dielectric materials have become indispensable in the field of materials science and engineering. Their unique properties, processing techniques, and diverse applications make them vital components in various electrical and electronic systems. Engineers working in this field must have a solid understanding of dielectric materials to design and develop innovative solutions for modern engineering challenges.

Magnetic Materials

Magnetic materials play a crucial role in various fields of engineering, from electronics and telecommunications to renewable energy and medical devices. Understanding the properties and applications of magnetic materials is essential for engineers working in the field of materials science and engineering. This subchapter aims to provide a comprehensive overview of magnetic materials, their characteristics, and their diverse applications.

Properties of Magnetic Materials: Magnetic materials possess unique properties that make them integral to numerous technological advancements. One of the key characteristics of these materials is their ability to generate a magnetic field, which arises due to the alignment of their atomic or molecular magnetic moments. This property allows for the manipulation of magnetic fields for a wide range of applications.

Classification of Magnetic Materials: Magnetic materials can be classified into three main categories: ferromagnetic, paramagnetic, and diamagnetic. Ferromagnetic materials, such as iron, nickel, and cobalt, have strong magnetic properties and can retain their magnetization even after the external magnetic field is removed. Paramagnetic materials, like aluminum and platinum, exhibit weak magnetic properties and only become magnetic when subjected to an external magnetic field. Diamagnetic materials, such as copper and bismuth, have a tendency to repel magnetic fields and display the weakest magnetic properties.

Applications of Magnetic Materials: The applications of magnetic materials are far-reaching and diverse. In the field of electronics, magnetic materials are used in the production of memory storage devices, such as hard drives and magnetic tapes. The use of magnetic materials in power generation and transmission systems is also widespread. Permanent magnets, made from materials like neodymium and samarium cobalt, are vital components in electric motors and generators. Magnetic materials also find applications in medical devices, such as magnetic resonance imaging (MRI) machines, where their magnetic properties aid in the visualization of internal body structures.

Advancements in Magnetic Materials: Recent advancements in magnetic materials have led to the development of new materials with enhanced magnetic properties. For instance, the discovery of rare-earth magnets, which possess exceptional magnetic strength, has revolutionized various industries. Researchers are also exploring the potential of magnetic nanoparticles for targeted drug delivery and cancer treatment.

In conclusion, magnetic materials are essential components in numerous engineering applications. Understanding the properties and applications of magnetic materials is crucial for engineers working in the field of materials science and engineering. This subchapter provides a comprehensive overview of magnetic materials, their properties, and their diverse applications in various industries. By delving into the exciting advancements in magnetic materials, engineers can harness their potential for future technological innovations.

Chapter 6: Phase Diagrams and Phase Transformations

Phase Diagrams

Phase diagrams play a crucial role in the field of Materials Science and Engineering, providing engineers with invaluable insights into the behavior and properties of materials under different conditions. These diagrams are graphical representations of the relationships between temperature, pressure, and the various phases or states of a material. By understanding phase diagrams, engineers can make informed decisions about the processing and application of engineering materials.

The subchapter on Phase Diagrams aims to provide engineers with a comprehensive overview of this essential tool. It begins by introducing the concept of phases and the importance of phase transformations in engineering materials. Engineers will learn about the different types of phase diagrams, including binary, ternary, and multicomponent phase diagrams, and how they are constructed.

The content then delves into the key components of phase diagrams. Engineers will explore the axes of temperature and composition, understanding how changes in these variables affect the phases present in a material. The subchapter explains the significance of phase boundaries, including solidus, liquidus, and solvus lines, and how they impact material behavior.

Furthermore, engineers will gain insights into the various phases commonly encountered in engineering materials, such as solid solutions, eutectics, and peritectics. The subchapter discusses the characteristics of these phases and their implications for material properties and processing techniques.

Phase diagrams are not static; they can be altered by changes in temperature, pressure, or composition. The content addresses the concept of phase equilibria and how it relates to phase diagrams. Engineers will learn about phase transformations, including melting, solidification, and solid-state transformations, and how they are represented in phase diagrams.

To aid engineers in their understanding and interpretation of phase diagrams, the subchapter provides practical examples and case studies. These real-world applications demonstrate how phase diagrams can be used to optimize material properties, design alloys, and control microstructural characteristics.

In conclusion, the subchapter on Phase Diagrams serves as an essential guide for engineers in the field of Materials Science and Engineering. By mastering the principles and applications of phase diagrams, engineers will be equipped with the knowledge and tools necessary to make informed decisions regarding material selection, processing, and applications.

Phase Transformations

In the field of materials science and engineering, understanding phase transformations is crucial for the design and development of new materials with enhanced properties. Phase transformations refer to the changes in the arrangement of atoms or molecules within a material, resulting in different phases or structures.

The study of phase transformations is essential as it allows engineers to manipulate and control the properties of materials to meet specific requirements. By understanding the underlying mechanisms of phase transformations, engineers can tailor materials for various applications, including automotive, aerospace, electronics, and biomedical industries.

One common type of phase transformation is solidification, which occurs when a liquid material cools and transforms into a solid state. This process is widely used in casting and additive manufacturing techniques, where molten metals or alloys are solidified into desired shapes. The structure and properties of the resulting solid material depend on the cooling rate and composition, making phase transformations a critical aspect of materials processing.

Another important phase transformation is the precipitation of a second phase within a material. This occurs when a solid solution undergoes a change in composition or temperature, causing the formation of a new phase. Precipitation hardening is a well-known example of this phenomenon, where small particles are dispersed within a metal matrix, enhancing its strength and hardness. This technique is commonly employed in the production of high-strength alloys used in structural applications.

Phase transformations can also occur in polymers, leading to changes in their physical and mechanical properties. For instance, the process of polymer crystallization involves the arrangement of polymer chains into an ordered structure, resulting in improved strength and stiffness. Engineers can optimize the crystallization process to enhance the performance of polymers in diverse applications, such as packaging, textiles, and medical devices.

Understanding phase transformations requires a combination of theoretical knowledge and experimental techniques. Engineers utilize various analytical tools, such as X-ray diffraction and electron microscopy, to observe and characterize the microstructure of materials undergoing phase transformations. Computational modeling and simulation techniques also play a crucial role in predicting and understanding the behavior of materials during phase transformations.

In conclusion, phase transformations are fundamental to the field of materials science and engineering. By studying and manipulating these transformations, engineers can tailor the properties of materials to meet specific requirements for a wide range of applications. The understanding of phase transformations allows for the development of innovative materials with enhanced strength, durability, and functionality, contributing to advancements in various industries.

Diffusion

Diffusion is a fundamental concept in materials science and engineering, playing a crucial role in understanding the behavior and properties of various engineering materials. This subchapter aims to provide engineers, particularly those in the field of materials science and engineering, with a comprehensive overview of diffusion and its significance in the processing and application of different materials.

Diffusion refers to the spontaneous movement of atoms or molecules from regions of high concentration to regions of low concentration. It occurs due to the inherent thermal energy possessed by particles, leading to their random motion. Understanding diffusion is essential for engineers as it impacts various material properties, including mechanical strength, electrical conductivity, and chemical reactivity.

The subchapter begins by introducing the basic principles of diffusion, such as Fick's laws, which describe the motion of atoms in solid-state materials. It explores the mechanisms of diffusion, including interstitial and substitutional diffusion, as well as vacancy diffusion. The role of defects in materials, such as grain boundaries and dislocations, in facilitating diffusion is also discussed.

Next, the subchapter delves into the practical applications of diffusion in engineering materials. It explores how diffusion influences processes like heat treatment, surface hardening, and alloying. Engineers will gain insights into how diffusion can be manipulated to enhance the desired properties of materials, such as the diffusion of carbon into steel to increase its hardness.

Furthermore, the subchapter addresses diffusion in different material systems, including metals, ceramics, and polymers. It highlights the unique diffusion behavior exhibited by each material class and how engineers can tailor diffusion processes to achieve desired outcomes. For instance, diffusion in ceramics is typically slower due to the presence of strong atomic bonds, while polymers exhibit higher diffusion coefficients due to their amorphous nature.

To provide a holistic understanding, the subchapter also covers advanced topics related to diffusion, such as diffusion in nanomaterials, diffusion-controlled reactions, and diffusion in complex systems. It discusses cutting-edge techniques used to study diffusion, including diffusion couple experiments and computational modeling.

Overall, this subchapter on diffusion is a valuable resource for engineers in the field of materials science and engineering. By comprehending the principles and applications of diffusion, engineers can optimize material processing techniques, design materials with enhanced properties, and develop innovative solutions for various engineering challenges.

Chapter 7: Materials Processing Techniques

Casting

Casting is a fundamental process in the field of materials science and engineering, with a wide range of applications in various industries. This subchapter aims to provide engineers with a comprehensive understanding of casting, its principles, and its role in manufacturing processes.

Casting is the process of shaping molten material into a desired form by pouring it into a mold and allowing it to solidify. This technique is particularly useful for producing complex shapes that may be difficult or costly to fabricate by other means. It is commonly used in the production of components for automotive, aerospace, and construction industries, among others.

The subchapter begins by introducing the different types of casting processes, including sand casting, investment casting, die casting, and continuous casting. Each method has its own advantages and limitations, and engineers must carefully select the appropriate process based on factors such as cost, desired properties, and production volume.

The next section explores the materials used in casting, with a focus on metals and alloys. It discusses the importance of selecting materials with suitable melting points, fluidity, and solidification behavior to achieve desired properties in the final product. The subchapter also covers the various techniques employed to control the solidification process and minimize defects such as porosity, shrinkage, and hot tears.

Furthermore, the subchapter delves into the design considerations for casting, including the design of the mold, gating system, and risers. It emphasizes the importance of proper design to ensure uniform cooling and solidification, as well as to prevent the formation of defects.

Other topics covered in the subchapter include the principles of heat transfer during casting, the use of computer simulations to optimize casting processes, and the post-casting treatments such as heat treatment and surface finishing.

Overall, this subchapter on casting equips engineers with the knowledge and understanding necessary to effectively utilize casting processes in their work. It emphasizes the importance of material selection, design considerations, and process optimization to achieve high-quality cast components. By mastering these concepts, engineers can enhance their ability to design and manufacture complex parts, contributing to advancements in materials science and engineering.

Forming

In the realm of materials science and engineering, the process of forming plays a crucial role in shaping and transforming various materials into functional components and structures. Forming refers to the techniques and methods used to change the shape, size, or properties of a material through mechanical or thermal means. These techniques are employed to create products that meet the desired specifications and requirements in a wide range of industries.

One of the primary goals of forming is to enhance the mechanical properties of a material while maintaining its integrity. Engineers must carefully select the appropriate forming method for a particular material to achieve the desired results. Common forming processes include casting, forging, rolling, extrusion, and sheet metal forming, each with its unique advantages and limitations.

Casting is a widely used forming technique that involves pouring molten metal into a mold, where it solidifies and takes on the desired shape. This process allows for the creation of complex geometries and is commonly used in the automotive and aerospace industries. Forging, on the other hand, involves the application of compressive forces to reshape a material by heating it to a specific temperature. This process enhances the material's strength and improves its grain structure, making it suitable for applications in heavy machinery and construction.

Rolling is a forming technique that involves passing a material between two or more rollers to reduce its thickness or change its shape. This process is commonly used in the production of sheet metal, as well as in the manufacturing of pipes, tubes, and rails. Extrusion, on the other hand, is a process where a material is forced through a die to produce long, continuous shapes with a fixed cross-sectional profile. This method is often used in the production of aluminum and plastic products.

Sheet metal forming encompasses a variety of techniques, including bending, deep drawing, and stretch forming, which are used to shape flat sheets of metal into three-dimensional components. These processes are widely employed in the manufacturing of automotive body panels, aircraft parts, and household appliances.

In conclusion, forming is an essential aspect of materials science and engineering, enabling engineers to shape and transform various materials into functional components and structures. By carefully selecting the appropriate forming techniques, engineers can enhance the mechanical properties of materials and meet the desired specifications and requirements of different industries.

Machining

Machining: Precision Craftsmanship for Engineering Materials

In the realm of Materials Science and Engineering, one crucial aspect that engineers must master is machining. This subchapter delves into the art and science of machining, exploring its importance, techniques, and applications in various industries. Whether you are a budding engineer or a seasoned professional, understanding the intricacies of machining is essential for producing high-quality components and products.

1. Introduction to Machining: Machining encompasses various processes that shape and alter materials to meet specific design requirements. From cutting, drilling, and milling to grinding, turning, and shaping, engineers employ a range of techniques to transform raw materials into precision-crafted components. This section provides a comprehensive overview of the machining process, highlighting its significance in manufacturing and fabrication.

2. Machining Techniques: This section delves into the fundamental techniques employed in machining. It covers the principles of cutting, tool selection, and machine setup. Engineers will learn about conventional machining methods, such as turning, milling, and drilling, as well as advanced techniques like electrical discharge machining (EDM) and laser cutting. Detailed explanations of each technique, accompanied by diagrams and case studies, equip readers with a solid understanding of their applications and limitations.

3. Machining Materials: Choosing the appropriate material for machining is crucial to achieve desired results. This section explores the properties of various engineering materials, including metals, polymers, ceramics, and composites, and their machinability. Engineers will learn how different materials respond to cutting forces, heat generation, and tool wear, enabling them to make informed decisions when selecting materials for specific applications.

4. Machining Processes and Applications: This section delves into the diverse applications of machining processes across industries. From aerospace and automotive to medical and electronics, engineers will discover how machining plays a vital role in fabricating intricate components and structures. The subchapter will also explore the challenges and advancements in machining technologies, such as computer numerical control (CNC) machining and additive manufacturing.

5. Machining Optimization: To maximize efficiency and minimize costs, engineers must optimize machining processes. This section provides insights into the factors influencing machining productivity, such as cutting parameters, tool life, and surface quality. It also discusses strategies for process optimization, including tool path planning, tool material selection, and coolant usage.

6. Future Trends in Machining: As technology advances, machining continues to evolve. This final section highlights emerging trends and innovations in machining, such as hybrid machining, nanomachining, and artificial intelligence-

driven machining. Engineers will gain a glimpse into the future of machining and its potential impact on the materials science and engineering field.

In conclusion, this subchapter on machining equips engineers with the knowledge and skills necessary to excel in the field of materials science and engineering. By understanding the principles, techniques, and applications of machining, engineers can harness its power to transform raw materials into precision-engineered components that drive innovation across industries.

Welding

Welding is a widely used and critical process in the field of materials science and engineering. It involves joining two or more pieces of metal or thermoplastic materials together to create a strong and durable bond. This subchapter will provide engineers with an in-depth understanding of the welding process, its various techniques, and its applications in different industries.

Firstly, the subchapter will delve into the fundamentals of welding, including the principles of metallurgy and the behavior of materials during the welding process. Engineers will gain insights into the various types of welding techniques, such as arc welding, resistance welding, and laser welding. Each technique will be explained in detail, highlighting its advantages, limitations, and suitable applications.

Furthermore, the subchapter will cover the factors that engineers need to consider when selecting the appropriate welding method for a specific application. These factors include the type of materials being welded, joint design, welding positions, and the desired mechanical properties of the final product. By understanding these considerations, engineers will be able to make informed decisions and ensure successful welding outcomes.

The subchapter will also address the challenges and potential defects associated with welding, such as distortion, residual stress, and the formation of undesired microstructures. Engineers will learn about various strategies and techniques to mitigate these issues, ensuring the production of high-quality welds.

Additionally, the subchapter will explore the advancements in welding technology, including automation and robotics. Engineers will gain insights into the latest welding equipment and their integration with computer-aided design (CAD) and computer-aided manufacturing (CAM) systems. The applications of welding in industries such as automotive, aerospace, construction, and energy will be highlighted, showcasing the significant impact of welding on various engineering sectors.

Overall, this subchapter on welding will equip engineers in the field of materials science and engineering with the necessary knowledge and skills to effectively utilize welding techniques. By understanding the principles, techniques, challenges, and advancements in welding, engineers will be able to make informed decisions during the design and manufacturing process, resulting in superior quality products and efficient production processes.

Heat Treatment

Heat treatment is a crucial process in the field of materials science and engineering. It involves the controlled heating and cooling of materials to alter their physical and mechanical properties. This subchapter will provide engineers with an in-depth understanding of the principles, techniques, and applications of heat treatment.

The primary objective of heat treatment is to enhance the performance and durability of materials. By subjecting them to specific heating and cooling cycles, engineers can modify their microstructure, which directly influences their mechanical, electrical, and thermal properties. Heat treatment can improve a material's hardness, strength, toughness, ductility, and corrosion resistance, making it suitable for various engineering applications.

The subchapter will begin by discussing the fundamental principles of heat treatment. It will cover the basic concepts of temperature, heating rate, soak time, and cooling rate, and their effects on the material's microstructure. Engineers will learn about phase transformations, such as annealing, quenching, tempering, and precipitation hardening, and how they can be controlled to achieve desired material properties.

Next, the subchapter will delve into the various heat treatment techniques commonly used in materials science and engineering. Engineers will gain insight into processes like normalizing, hardening, case hardening, and surface hardening. The subchapter will explain the procedures, equipment, and parameters involved in each technique, allowing engineers to select the most suitable method for their specific application.

Furthermore, the subchapter will explore the applications of heat treatment in different industries. Engineers will learn how heat treatment is used to manufacture components for automotive, aerospace, construction, and energy sectors. They will understand the importance of heat treatment in enhancing the performance of steels, aluminum alloys, titanium alloys, and other materials used in these industries.

Throughout the subchapter, engineers will find practical examples, case studies, and illustrations that demonstrate the real-world applications of heat treatment. They will also be introduced to advanced heat treatment techniques, such as laser heating, induction heating, and surface modification, which are gaining prominence in modern engineering.

By the end of this subchapter, engineers specializing in materials science and engineering will have a comprehensive understanding of heat treatment. They will be equipped with the knowledge and skills to design, optimize, and control heat treatment processes to achieve desired material properties for various applications.

Surface Treatment

Surface treatment is a crucial aspect of materials science and engineering, as it directly influences the performance, durability, and aesthetic appeal of various engineering components and products. This subchapter explores the importance of surface treatment, different techniques employed, and their applications in the field of engineering.

The primary objective of surface treatment is to modify the surface properties of a material to enhance its functionality and performance. Surface treatments can improve corrosion resistance, wear resistance, hardness, adhesion, and even alter the appearance of the material. Engineers employ various techniques to achieve these desired modifications, depending on the material and the intended application.

One commonly used surface treatment technique is coating. Coatings provide a protective layer on the surface of a material, shielding it from environmental factors such as moisture, chemicals, and abrasion. Different types of coatings, such as metallic, ceramic, and polymer-based coatings, are used based on the specific requirements of the application. Coatings can also be used to improve the visual appeal of a product, making it more attractive to consumers.

Another widely employed surface treatment method is surface modification through heat treatment. Heat treatment involves subjecting a material to controlled heating and cooling processes to alter its microstructure and, consequently, its properties. This technique is commonly used to improve the hardness, toughness, and strength of metallic materials. Heat treatment processes include annealing, quenching, tempering, and case hardening.

Surface treatment also encompasses processes like shot peening, polishing, and grinding. Shot peening involves bombarding the surface of a material with small metallic or ceramic particles to induce compressive stresses, thereby improving fatigue resistance. Polishing and grinding are mechanical processes that achieve a smooth and reflective surface finish, important for applications in optics, automotive, and consumer electronics.

In addition to these techniques, surface treatment can also involve surface engineering processes such as plasma spraying, ion implantation, and chemical vapor deposition. These techniques are used to modify the surface composition and structure of a material, often to enhance its wear resistance, hardness, or to impart specific properties such as biocompatibility or superhydrophobicity.

In conclusion, surface treatment plays a pivotal role in materials science and engineering. It allows engineers to modify the surface properties of materials to meet specific requirements and enhance performance. Coating, heat treatment, mechanical processes, and surface engineering methods are some of the techniques employed in surface treatment. Understanding and utilizing these techniques are essential for engineers to design and develop materials with improved functionality, durability, and aesthetic appeal.

Chapter 8: Metals and Alloys

Ferrous Metals and Alloys

Introduction:
Ferrous metals and alloys have played a crucial role in the field of materials science and engineering for centuries. This subchapter aims to provide engineers with a comprehensive understanding of the properties, processing, and applications of these materials. From their historical significance to their modern-day applications, this subchapter delves into the world of ferrous metals and alloys.

Historical Significance:
Ferrous metals, primarily iron and its alloys, have been utilized by various civilizations throughout history. From the Iron Age to the Industrial Revolution, these materials have shaped the course of human development. Engineers need to comprehend the historical significance to appreciate the evolution of ferrous metals and their impact on modern engineering practices.

Properties of Ferrous Metals and Alloys:
Ferrous metals possess distinct properties that make them invaluable in engineering applications. This subchapter explores these properties, including high strength, excellent ductility, and superior magnetic properties. The subchapter also discusses the effects of alloying elements and heat treatment on the properties of ferrous metals, enabling engineers to tailor these materials to specific requirements.

Processing Techniques:
Understanding the processing techniques is essential for engineers

working with ferrous metals and alloys. This subchapter provides a comprehensive overview of various processing techniques, such as casting, forging, and heat treatment. It highlights the importance of each technique and its impact on the final properties and microstructure of the material.

Applications in Engineering:
Ferrous metals and alloys find extensive applications in a wide range of engineering fields. This subchapter explores their use in structural applications, machinery, automotive industry, aerospace, and more. It also discusses the advantages and limitations of using ferrous metals in different engineering applications, helping engineers make informed decisions when selecting materials for their projects.

Emerging Trends and Future Prospects:
This subchapter concludes with a discussion on the emerging trends and future prospects of ferrous metals and alloys in the field of materials science and engineering. It highlights the ongoing research and development efforts aimed at enhancing the properties and performance of these materials. Engineers will gain insights into the potential advancements and opportunities that lie ahead in the world of ferrous metals and alloys.

Conclusion:
Ferrous metals and alloys continue to be vital materials in the field of materials science and engineering. This subchapter provides engineers with a comprehensive understanding of their properties, processing techniques, applications, and future prospects. By mastering this knowledge, engineers can make informed decisions and leverage the

potential of ferrous metals and alloys in their projects, contributing to the advancement of the field.

Non-ferrous Metals and Alloys

Non-ferrous metals and alloys play a crucial role in various industries and engineering applications. Unlike ferrous metals that contain iron, non-ferrous metals do not contain iron as their primary element. This subchapter explores the properties, processing techniques, and applications of non-ferrous metals and alloys, providing engineers in the field of materials science and engineering with a comprehensive understanding of these materials.

One of the most commonly used non-ferrous metals is aluminum. Its low density, high strength, and excellent corrosion resistance make it highly desirable for a wide range of applications. Engineers rely on aluminum and its alloys for aerospace components, automobile parts, packaging materials, and electrical conductors. Understanding the various alloying elements and heat treatment processes that can be used to modify the properties of aluminum is essential for engineers working with this versatile metal.

Copper and its alloys are also extensively used in engineering applications. Copper possesses excellent electrical and thermal conductivity, making it indispensable in electrical and electronic industries. Copper alloys, such as bronze and brass, offer enhanced strength and corrosion resistance, enabling their use in plumbing fixtures, musical instruments, and marine applications. Engineers need to understand the composition, processing, and properties of copper and its alloys to select the most suitable material for their specific applications.

Another important group of non-ferrous metals is the precious metals, including gold, silver, and platinum. These metals are valued for their rarity, high electrical conductivity, and resistance to corrosion. Engineers working in specialized fields, such as electronics, jewelry, and chemical engineering, need to comprehend the unique properties and processing techniques associated with these precious metals.

In addition to the individual non-ferrous metals, engineers must also be familiar with various non-ferrous alloys, such as titanium alloys and nickel-based alloys. These alloys offer exceptional strength-to-weight ratios, excellent corrosion resistance, and high-temperature capabilities. Their applications range from aircraft components to medical implants, demanding a thorough understanding of their composition, processing, and mechanical properties.

By studying non-ferrous metals and alloys in depth, engineers in the field of materials science and engineering can make informed decisions on material selection, processing techniques, and design considerations. This subchapter serves as a valuable resource, providing essential knowledge to enhance the understanding and application of non-ferrous metals and alloys in various engineering fields.

Metal Matrix Composites

Metal Matrix Composites (MMCs) are advanced materials that have found widespread applications in the field of materials science and engineering. These composites consist of a metal matrix reinforced with one or more secondary phases, such as ceramic or metallic particles, fibers, or whiskers. The combination of the metal matrix and the reinforcing phase(s) imparts enhanced mechanical, thermal, and electrical properties to the composite material, making it suitable for a wide range of engineering applications.

One of the key advantages of MMCs is their superior strength-to-weight ratio. The addition of the reinforcing phase(s) significantly improves the mechanical properties of the metal matrix, allowing the composite to withstand higher loads and stresses compared to conventional metals. This makes MMCs particularly suitable for applications where weight reduction is critical, such as in the aerospace and automotive industries.

In addition to their high strength, MMCs also exhibit excellent wear resistance and thermal stability. The reinforcing phase(s) act as barriers, preventing the propagation of cracks and reducing the wear rate of the material. This makes MMCs ideal for applications that require resistance to abrasive wear, such as cutting tools, engine components, and wear-resistant coatings.

Furthermore, MMCs can exhibit tailored thermal and electrical conductivity properties. By selecting the appropriate reinforcing phase(s) and controlling their volume fraction, engineers can design composites with specific thermal and electrical properties. This makes

MMCs suitable for applications that require efficient heat dissipation, such as heat sinks in electronic devices, as well as electrical contacts and connectors.

The processing of MMCs involves various techniques, such as powder metallurgy, casting, and in-situ synthesis. Each technique offers advantages and limitations in terms of cost, complexity, and the types of composites that can be produced. Engineers need to carefully consider the processing method based on the desired properties, cost-effectiveness, and scalability of production.

In conclusion, Metal Matrix Composites offer a vast range of possibilities for engineers in the field of materials science and engineering. With their exceptional mechanical, thermal, and electrical properties, MMCs have become indispensable in industries that demand high-performance materials. By understanding the processing methods and tailoring the composition, engineers can harness the full potential of MMCs to meet the ever-increasing demands of modern technology and design.

Shape Memory Alloys

Shape memory alloys (SMAs) are a unique class of materials that have gained significant attention in the field of materials science and engineering. These alloys possess the remarkable ability to remember their original shape and return to it after being deformed. This unique property, known as shape memory effect, is a result of the material's ability to undergo a reversible phase transformation between two different crystal structures.

SMAs are typically composed of a combination of nickel, titanium, and other elements such as copper, palladium, or iron. The most commonly used SMA is known as Nitinol (a combination of nickel and titanium). The phase transformation responsible for the shape memory effect occurs between a high-temperature phase (austenite) and a low-temperature phase (martensite).

The shape memory effect in SMAs can be activated through different means, including temperature change, mechanical stress, or a combination of both. When the SMA is heated above a certain temperature called the transformation temperature, it reverts from the low-temperature martensite phase to the high-temperature austenite phase, recovering its original shape. Conversely, when the SMA is cooled below the transformation temperature, it transforms back to the martensite phase and can be easily deformed.

The unique characteristics of SMAs make them suitable for a wide range of applications. One common application is in the biomedical field, where SMAs are used in orthodontic wires, stents, and surgical instruments. The shape memory effect allows these devices to adapt to the patient's body temperature and apply the necessary force or shape.

SMAs also find applications in the aerospace and automotive industries. In aerospace, SMA actuators are used for various purposes, including wing morphing and vibration damping. In the automotive industry, SMAs are utilized in smart materials for automotive systems, such as smart springs, smart dampers, and smart tires, to improve vehicle performance and safety.

In conclusion, shape memory alloys are an exciting and versatile class of materials that exhibit unique properties. Their ability to remember and recover their original shape after deformation has led to applications in various fields, including biomedical, aerospace, and automotive industries. As engineers, understanding the properties and behavior of SMAs can open up new possibilities for designing advanced and innovative materials and systems.

Chapter 9: Polymers and Composites

Polymers: Structure and Properties

Introduction:
In the field of materials science and engineering, polymers play a crucial role due to their diverse applications in various industries. Understanding the structure and properties of polymers is essential for engineers working with materials to design and develop innovative products. This subchapter aims to provide a comprehensive overview of the structure and properties of polymers, equipping engineers with the knowledge required to make informed decisions when selecting and working with these materials.

Polymer Structure:
Polymers are large molecules composed of repeating subunits called monomers. The arrangement of these monomers determines the polymer's structure and subsequent properties. The subchapter will delve into the three primary polymer structures: linear, branched, and cross-linked. It will explore the effects of molecular weight, chain length, and branching on the mechanical, thermal, and chemical properties of polymers.

Polymer Properties:
The properties of polymers make them highly versatile materials suitable for a wide range of applications. This section will discuss key properties such as mechanical strength, flexibility, durability, thermal stability, electrical conductivity, and optical properties. Engineers will gain a deep understanding of how the structure of polymers influences

these properties, enabling them to make informed decisions regarding material selection for specific applications.

Polymer Processing:
Engineers in materials science and engineering must also understand the processing techniques involved in working with polymers. This subchapter will introduce various polymer processing methods, including injection molding, extrusion, blow molding, and thermoforming. The influence of processing techniques on the structure and properties of polymers will be highlighted, emphasizing the importance of optimizing processing parameters to achieve desired material characteristics.

Polymer Applications:
The final section of this subchapter will explore the wide-ranging applications of polymers in industries such as automotive, aerospace, electronics, packaging, and biomedical engineering. Engineers will gain insights into how the structure and properties of polymers make them ideal for specific applications, such as high-performance composites, lightweight materials, electrical insulation, and biocompatible implants.

Conclusion:
Understanding the structure and properties of polymers is vital for engineers in materials science and engineering. This subchapter provides a comprehensive overview of polymer structures, properties, processing techniques, and applications. By gaining knowledge in this area, engineers will be equipped to select and manipulate polymers effectively, leading to the development of innovative materials and products across various industries.

Polymer Processing

In the field of materials science and engineering, polymer processing plays a crucial role in shaping and transforming raw polymer materials into useful products. This subchapter aims to provide engineers with a comprehensive understanding of the various techniques and processes involved in polymer processing, highlighting their significance in industrial applications.

Polymer processing involves a series of operations that convert polymer resins into finished products. These operations include compounding, extrusion, molding, and casting, among others. Each process involves specific parameters, such as temperature, pressure, and shear rate, which significantly influence the final product's properties and performance.

Compounding is the first step in polymer processing, where different additives, fillers, and reinforcements are mixed with the polymer resin to enhance its properties. This process is crucial in achieving the desired characteristics, such as improved strength, durability, and thermal stability, making the polymer suitable for specific applications.

Extrusion is a widely used technique in polymer processing, where the molten polymer is forced through a die to form continuous profiles or sheets. This process is commonly employed in the production of pipes, films, and fibers. Engineers must carefully control the extrusion parameters, such as temperature, screw speed, and die design, to ensure the desired shape and dimensions of the final product.

Molding is another essential polymer processing technique, involving the shaping of polymer resins into specific forms using heat and pressure. Injection molding, compression molding, and blow molding are commonly used methods, offering high production rates and excellent product consistency. This process is extensively utilized in the manufacturing of automotive components, consumer goods, and packaging materials.

Casting is a process used to produce intricate shapes and complex geometries using liquid polymer resins. It involves pouring the liquid resin into a mold, where it solidifies to form the desired shape. Casting is widely employed in the production of medical devices, electronic components, and aerospace parts.

Engineers involved in polymer processing must also consider the rheological behavior of polymers, which describes their flow properties under different conditions. Understanding rheology is crucial in optimizing processing parameters and ensuring quality control in polymer manufacturing.

In conclusion, polymer processing is a vital aspect of materials science and engineering, enabling the transformation of raw polymer materials into useful products. Engineers must possess a deep understanding of the various techniques and processes involved in polymer processing to meet the growing demands of industrial applications. By mastering the principles of compounding, extrusion, molding, casting, and rheology, engineers can create innovative polymer products that cater to specific niches and contribute to technological advancements in various industries.

Composite Materials: Types and Properties

Introduction:
In the field of materials science and engineering, composite materials have emerged as a game-changer. These materials, consisting of two or more distinct components, offer superior properties that cannot be achieved by any single material alone. This subchapter aims to delve into the types and properties of composite materials, providing engineers with an in-depth understanding of their applications and potential.

Types of Composite Materials:
Composite materials can be broadly classified into three categories: polymer matrix composites (PMCs), metal matrix composites (MMCs), and ceramic matrix composites (CMCs). PMCs are the most common type, comprising a polymer resin matrix reinforced with fibers such as carbon, glass, or aramid. MMCs, on the other hand, use a metal matrix with reinforcements like particles, whiskers, or fibers. CMCs employ a ceramic matrix reinforced with ceramic fibers or particles.

Properties and Advantages:
Composite materials exhibit a wide range of properties that make them highly desirable for various engineering applications. One of their key advantages is their exceptional strength-to-weight ratio, making them lightweight yet incredibly strong. This property is particularly beneficial in industries such as aerospace, where reducing weight is critical for fuel efficiency. Moreover, composites offer excellent corrosion resistance, thermal stability, and electrical

insulation properties, expanding their applications to fields like marine engineering and electronics.

Furthermore, composite materials possess tailorable properties, allowing engineers to customize them according to specific requirements. Through careful selection of matrix, reinforcement, and manufacturing processes, composites can be engineered to be stiffer, more flexible, or have enhanced heat resistance. This versatility provides engineers with a wide range of design possibilities and allows for the creation of materials that can withstand extreme environments.

Applications:
The ever-growing applications of composite materials span across numerous industries. In aerospace, composites are extensively used in aircraft structures, reducing weight and enhancing fuel efficiency. In automotive engineering, composites find applications in body panels, reducing vehicle weight and increasing fuel economy. Additionally, composites are used in sports equipment, construction materials, wind turbine blades, and medical devices, among others.

Conclusion:
In conclusion, composite materials have revolutionized the field of materials science and engineering. Their unique combination of properties, including strength, lightweight, corrosion resistance, and tailorable characteristics, make them invaluable for numerous applications. Understanding the different types and properties of composites is crucial for engineers in the materials science and engineering niche, enabling them to harness the full potential of these remarkable materials.

Fiber Reinforced Composites

Fiber reinforced composites are a class of materials that combine the desirable properties of both the reinforcing fibers and the matrix material. These materials have gained immense popularity in various fields of engineering, including aerospace, automotive, and civil engineering, due to their exceptional mechanical properties, lightweight nature, and high strength-to-weight ratio.

In fiber reinforced composites, the reinforcing fibers are embedded within a matrix material, which can be a polymer, metal, or ceramic. The fibers are typically strong and stiff, such as carbon fibers, glass fibers, or aramid fibers, while the matrix material acts as a binding agent, providing support and protecting the fibers from external damage.

The choice of fibers and matrix material depends on the specific application and desired properties of the composite. For example, carbon fiber reinforced composites are widely used in aerospace applications due to their excellent strength and low weight. On the other hand, glass fiber reinforced composites find application in construction and automotive industries due to their cost-effectiveness and good mechanical properties.

The manufacturing process of fiber reinforced composites involves several steps, including fiber selection, fiber orientation, and impregnation of the fibers with the matrix material. Various techniques, such as hand lay-up, filament winding, and resin transfer molding, are used to create the desired fiber orientation and ensure proper bonding between the fibers and matrix.

One of the key advantages of fiber reinforced composites is their high strength-to-weight ratio. These materials exhibit superior mechanical properties, such as high tensile strength, stiffness, and resistance to fatigue and impact. As a result, they can withstand heavy loads and harsh environmental conditions without undergoing significant deformation or failure. This makes them ideal for applications where weight reduction is crucial, such as aircraft components, wind turbine blades, and sports equipment.

Furthermore, fiber reinforced composites offer excellent corrosion resistance, electrical insulation, and thermal stability. They are also highly customizable, allowing engineers to tailor their properties based on specific requirements. However, these materials also have some limitations, such as high manufacturing costs, difficulty in recycling, and susceptibility to delamination under certain conditions.

In conclusion, fiber reinforced composites are versatile materials with a wide range of applications in engineering. Their exceptional properties make them highly desirable for industries seeking lightweight, high-strength materials. With ongoing advancements in materials science and engineering, fiber reinforced composites are expected to play an increasingly vital role in shaping the future of various industries.

Polymer Matrix Composites

Polymer matrix composites (PMCs) are a class of materials that have gained significant importance in various engineering applications. This subchapter aims to provide engineers, particularly those in the field of materials science and engineering, with a comprehensive understanding of PMCs, including their properties, processing techniques, and wide-ranging applications.

PMCs consist of a polymer matrix, which acts as a binder, reinforced with high-strength fibers or particles. The combination of the matrix and reinforcement imparts unique mechanical, thermal, and electrical properties to these composites, making them highly desirable for a multitude of applications. One of the key advantages of PMCs is their lightweight nature, which allows for enhanced fuel efficiency and performance in industries such as aerospace, automotive, and sports equipment.

In this subchapter, engineers will explore the different types of polymer matrices, including thermosetting and thermoplastic polymers, and their respective advantages and limitations. The selection of an appropriate matrix is crucial as it determines the overall performance and processing methods of the composite. Furthermore, engineers will gain insights into various reinforcement materials, such as carbon fibers, glass fibers, and nanoparticles, and their impact on the final composite's properties.

The processing techniques for PMCs are diverse and can range from simple hand lay-up methods to advanced automated manufacturing processes like filament winding and resin transfer molding. Engineers will learn about the advantages and limitations of each technique, enabling them to select the most suitable method based on the desired characteristics of the final composite.

The subchapter also delves into the mechanical behavior of PMCs, including their strength, stiffness, and toughness. Engineers will gain an understanding of how the selection of matrix and reinforcement materials, as well as the processing techniques, influence these mechanical properties. Additionally, the subchapter explores the thermal and electrical conductivity of PMCs, which are important considerations for applications in industries such as electronics and energy.

Finally, engineers will be introduced to a wide range of applications for PMCs, including aircraft components, automotive parts, sporting goods, and biomedical devices. Real-world case studies will highlight the successful utilization of PMCs in these industries, emphasizing the advantages they offer in terms of performance, weight reduction, and cost-effectiveness.

In conclusion, this subchapter on Polymer Matrix Composites provides engineers in the field of materials science and engineering with a comprehensive understanding of PMCs, from their properties and processing techniques to their wide-ranging applications. By delving into the intricacies of PMCs, engineers will be equipped with the knowledge to design and develop innovative solutions that meet the demands of modern engineering challenges.

Chapter 10: Ceramics and Glasses

Ceramic Materials: Structure and Properties

Introduction:
In the field of materials science and engineering, ceramic materials play a crucial role due to their unique properties and applications. This subchapter aims to provide engineers with an in-depth understanding of the structure and properties of ceramic materials, enabling them to make informed decisions when selecting and utilizing these materials in various engineering applications.

Structure of Ceramic Materials:
Ceramic materials are primarily composed of metallic and non-metallic elements, with a crystalline atomic structure. The subchapter will delve into the crystal structures of ceramics, explaining the arrangement of atoms and how it affects their properties. It will also discuss the presence of voids, grain boundaries, and defects in ceramic materials, emphasizing their influence on mechanical, electrical, and thermal behavior.

Properties of Ceramic Materials:
The properties of ceramic materials make them highly desirable for a wide range of engineering applications. This subchapter will explore the fundamental properties such as hardness, brittleness, high melting points, excellent thermal and electrical insulation, and chemical stability. Additionally, it will address the unique properties exhibited by specific ceramic materials, including piezoelectricity, ferroelectricity, superconductivity, and semiconductivity.

Mechanical Behavior: Understanding the mechanical behavior of ceramic materials is crucial when designing structures that can withstand different loads and environments. This subchapter will discuss the relationship between the crystal structure and mechanical properties such as strength, toughness, and fracture behavior. It will also cover the factors influencing fracture, including stress concentrations, crack propagation, and the role of grain boundaries.

Thermal and Electrical Behavior: Ceramic materials possess exceptional thermal and electrical properties, making them suitable for applications such as thermal insulation, high-temperature sensors, and electronic devices. The subchapter will delve into thermal conductivity, coefficient of thermal expansion, and thermal shock resistance. Furthermore, it will cover electrical conductivity and dielectric properties, including the concept of band gaps and their effect on electrical behavior.

Applications and Future Developments: To showcase the practical significance of ceramic materials, this subchapter will highlight their applications in various fields, including aerospace, automotive, electronics, and biomedical engineering. It will also discuss ongoing research and future developments in ceramic materials, such as advanced fabrication techniques, nanoceramics, and the incorporation of ceramics in cutting-edge technologies like fuel cells and batteries.

Conclusion:
Ceramic materials offer unique properties that make them indispensable in engineering applications. This subchapter aims to

equip engineers in the niche of materials science and engineering with a comprehensive understanding of the structure and properties of ceramic materials. By gaining knowledge in this area, engineers will be able to harness the capabilities of ceramics effectively and contribute to innovative solutions in their respective fields.

Traditional Ceramics

Traditional ceramics refer to a class of materials that have been used by humans for centuries due to their unique properties and versatility. In this subchapter, we will explore the characteristics, processing techniques, and applications of traditional ceramics, with a focus on their relevance to the field of materials science and engineering.

Traditional ceramics are primarily composed of inorganic nonmetallic compounds, such as clay minerals, silica, and feldspar. These materials are abundant in nature and can be easily shaped into various forms, making them ideal for a wide range of applications. One of the key properties of traditional ceramics is their high mechanical strength, which enables them to withstand high temperatures, pressures, and mechanical stresses. This makes them suitable for use in demanding environments, such as furnace linings, cutting tools, and refractory bricks.

The processing of traditional ceramics involves several steps, including raw material preparation, shaping, drying, and firing. The raw materials are first ground into a fine powder and mixed to achieve a desired composition. The resulting mixture, known as a ceramic body, is then shaped into the desired form using techniques such as molding, extrusion, or pressing. The shaped ceramic is then dried to remove any moisture, followed by firing at high temperatures to achieve the desired mechanical and thermal properties.

Traditional ceramics find applications in various industries, including construction, electronics, automotive, and healthcare. In the construction sector, ceramic tiles are widely used for their aesthetic appeal and durability. In the electronics industry, ceramics are used as insulating materials in electronic components and as substrates for integrated circuits. Additionally, traditional ceramics are used in automotive applications, such as engine components and exhaust systems, due to their high temperature resistance.

As materials science and engineering professionals, understanding the properties and processing techniques of traditional ceramics is crucial for designing and selecting appropriate materials for specific applications. By leveraging the unique properties of traditional ceramics, engineers can develop innovative solutions for a wide range of challenges.

In conclusion, traditional ceramics have played a vital role in human civilization for centuries. Their exceptional properties, such as high mechanical strength and temperature resistance, make them indispensable in various industries. By delving into the realm of traditional ceramics, engineers can unlock the potential of these materials to create novel solutions and contribute to the advancement of materials science and engineering.

Advanced Ceramics

Ceramics have been used for thousands of years due to their unique properties such as high strength, high melting points, and excellent electrical and thermal insulation. However, traditional ceramics often lacked the desired mechanical properties for many engineering applications. In recent years, advanced ceramics have emerged as a new class of materials with enhanced properties and improved performance, making them highly attractive for a wide range of industries.

This subchapter will delve into the fascinating field of advanced ceramics, exploring their properties, processing techniques, and applications. As engineers in the niche of Materials Science and Engineering, understanding the potential of advanced ceramics is crucial for developing innovative solutions to current technological challenges.

Properties of advanced ceramics are significantly different from those of traditional ceramics. Their exceptional hardness, low density, and excellent wear resistance make them ideal for applications in cutting tools, bearings, and armor materials. Moreover, advanced ceramics exhibit excellent chemical stability, corrosion resistance, and high-temperature resistance, making them suitable for use in harsh environments such as aerospace and energy industries.

The subchapter will also discuss the processing techniques employed to fabricate advanced ceramics. Unlike traditional ceramics, which are typically shaped through simple methods like molding and firing, advanced ceramics require more complex techniques such as powder synthesis, shaping, and sintering. These processes are crucial to achieving the desired microstructure and properties of advanced ceramics.

Furthermore, the subchapter will explore a wide range of applications where advanced ceramics have found success. From biomedical implants and dental prosthetics to electronic components and fuel cells, advanced ceramics have revolutionized various industries. Their unique combination of properties makes them ideal for cutting-edge applications that demand high performance and reliability.

Overall, this subchapter on advanced ceramics aims to provide engineers in the niche of Materials Science and Engineering with a comprehensive understanding of the exciting world of advanced ceramics. By exploring their properties, processing techniques, and applications, engineers will be able to harness the full potential of advanced ceramics to develop innovative solutions for future technological challenges.

Glass: Structure and Properties

Glass is a unique material that has found extensive applications in various engineering fields. Understanding its structure and properties is crucial for engineers in the niche of Materials Science and Engineering. This subchapter aims to provide an in-depth overview of the structure and properties of glass, shedding light on its remarkable characteristics and applications.

The structure of glass is amorphous, lacking long-range order like crystalline materials. It is primarily composed of silica (SiO_2) along with various additives to modify its properties. The random arrangement of atoms in glass gives it unique optical, thermal, and mechanical properties. Engineers must comprehend the structure-property relationship to design and optimize glass for specific applications.

One of the defining properties of glass is its transparency, allowing the transmission of visible light. This property makes it ideal for optical applications like lenses, windows, and display screens. Furthermore, glass exhibits excellent chemical stability, resisting corrosion from many substances. This makes it suitable for laboratory equipment, chemical storage containers, and even nuclear waste disposal.

The mechanical properties of glass are also noteworthy. It is inherently brittle due to the absence of a crystal lattice, making it susceptible to fractures under stress. However, advances in glass manufacturing techniques, such as tempering and laminating, have significantly improved its strength and durability. Engineers can now utilize glass in structural applications like facades, bridges, and even bulletproof windows.

Thermal properties of glass are critical in applications involving extreme temperatures. Its low thermal conductivity makes it an excellent insulator, making it invaluable in building materials to conserve energy. On the other hand, glass can withstand high temperatures without melting or deforming, making it suitable for ovenware, laboratory crucibles, and even spacecraft windows.

This subchapter will delve into the various types of glass, including soda-lime glass, borosilicate glass, and specialty glasses like tempered and laminated glass. It will also discuss the manufacturing processes involved in shaping glass, such as blowing, casting, and drawing.

In conclusion, the subchapter on "Glass: Structure and Properties" provides engineers in the niche of Materials Science and Engineering with a comprehensive understanding of the unique characteristics of glass. By exploring its structure and properties, engineers can leverage the versatility of glass in a wide range of applications, from optics and construction to chemical and thermal resistance.

Glass-Ceramics

Glass-ceramics are a unique class of materials that possess a combination of glassy and crystalline properties, making them highly versatile and desirable for various engineering applications. This subchapter will delve into the fundamental characteristics, processing techniques, and applications of glass-ceramics, providing engineers in the field of materials science and engineering with a comprehensive understanding of this fascinating material.

Glass-ceramics are derived from glasses that have been subjected to controlled thermal treatments, resulting in the nucleation and growth of crystalline phases within the glass matrix. This transformation imparts exceptional mechanical, thermal, and electrical properties to the material, surpassing those of conventional glasses. The ability to tailor the composition and processing conditions allows engineers to engineer the properties of glass-ceramics to meet specific application requirements, making them highly versatile in a wide range of industries.

The subchapter will explore the various methods of producing glass-ceramics, including controlled crystallization of glasses, devitrification, and controlled nucleation and growth techniques. Detailed discussions on the factors influencing the formation and growth of crystalline phases will be presented, enabling engineers to optimize the processing parameters for desired material properties.

Furthermore, the subchapter will highlight the outstanding properties of glass-ceramics, such as high strength, excellent thermal shock resistance, low thermal expansion coefficient, and good electrical insulation. These properties make glass-ceramics suitable for numerous applications, including cookware, dental restorations, electronic substrates, aerospace components, and nuclear waste immobilization.

Additionally, the subchapter will delve into the characterization techniques used to evaluate the microstructure, phase composition, and properties of glass-ceramics. X-ray diffraction, scanning electron microscopy, and differential thermal analysis are among the techniques covered, providing engineers with the necessary tools to assess and understand the behavior of glass-ceramics.

In conclusion, glass-ceramics are a unique class of materials that bridge the gap between glasses and ceramics, offering exceptional properties and versatility. This subchapter aims to equip engineers in the field of materials science and engineering with a comprehensive understanding of glass-ceramics, enabling them to design and select suitable materials for a wide range of applications. The knowledge gained from this subchapter will empower engineers to exploit the full potential of glass-ceramics in their pursuit of innovative and efficient engineering solutions.

Chapter 11: Materials Selection and Design

Material Selection Criteria

In the field of materials science and engineering, the selection of suitable materials for a particular application is a critical decision that engineers have to make. The success or failure of a product or structure often depends on the materials chosen. Therefore, it is essential to have a thorough understanding of the material selection criteria to ensure optimal performance, durability, and cost-effectiveness.

1. Mechanical Properties: One of the primary considerations in material selection is the mechanical properties of the materials. Engineers need to evaluate factors such as strength, toughness, hardness, and ductility to ensure that the material can withstand the expected loads and conditions without failure. The mechanical properties play a vital role in determining the performance and reliability of a component or structure.

2. Chemical Compatibility: The chemical environment in which a material will be exposed is another crucial criterion for selection. Compatibility with the surrounding chemicals, including acids, bases, solvents, and corrosive substances, is essential to prevent degradation, corrosion, or chemical reactions that could compromise the integrity of the material.

3. Thermal Properties: The ability of a material to withstand high or low temperatures is vital in various engineering applications. Thermal conductivity, coefficient of thermal expansion, and the ability to resist

thermal shock are important factors to consider when selecting materials for applications involving extreme temperature conditions.

4. Electrical Properties: In certain applications, electrical conductivity or insulating properties are critical factors. Materials with desired electrical properties, such as conductivity, resistivity, dielectric strength, and insulation properties, must be carefully selected to ensure optimal performance and safety.

5. Cost: Cost-effectiveness is a significant consideration in material selection. Engineers need to balance the performance requirements with the cost of materials, manufacturing processes, and maintenance. The availability and abundance of the material in the market also influence the cost factor.

6. Environmental Impact: With increasing concerns about sustainability and environmental impact, engineers must consider the ecological footprint of the materials they choose. Factors such as recyclability, energy consumption during manufacturing, and the overall environmental impact of the material's life cycle should be considered.

7. Manufacturing Constraints: The feasibility of manufacturing processes and the ease of fabrication are essential considerations in material selection. Engineers need to assess whether the chosen material can be readily shaped, joined, machined, or processed to meet the specific design requirements.

In conclusion, material selection criteria are crucial in ensuring the successful and efficient functioning of engineering components and structures. Engineers in the field of materials science and engineering must carefully evaluate mechanical, chemical, thermal, electrical properties, along with cost, environmental impact, and manufacturing constraints to make informed decisions. By considering these criteria, engineers can select materials that optimize performance, durability, and cost-effectiveness for a wide range of applications.

Design Constraints and Considerations

In the field of materials science and engineering, the design process plays a crucial role in the successful development of products and structures. Designing with engineering materials requires a deep understanding of their properties, processing techniques, and applications. However, it is equally important to consider the various design constraints that can significantly impact the final outcome.

One of the primary design constraints is the requirement for materials to withstand specific loads and forces. Engineers must carefully analyze the expected mechanical stresses and strains on a component to ensure that the selected materials possess the necessary strength and durability. Factors such as the material's yield strength, ultimate tensile strength, hardness, and fatigue resistance must be taken into account to prevent premature failures.

Another critical consideration is the environment in which the material will be used. Different materials exhibit varying degrees of resistance to temperature, humidity, chemicals, and corrosion. Engineers must evaluate the potential exposure of the material to these factors and select materials that can withstand them without compromising performance or safety.

Manufacturability is also a vital design constraint. The chosen materials must be compatible with the available processing techniques, such as casting, forging, machining, or additive manufacturing. Factors such as material formability, machinability, weldability, and surface finish requirements must be considered to ensure efficient and cost-effective production.

Design constraints often extend beyond the material itself. Size and weight limitations, aesthetics, and cost considerations are additional factors that engineers must take into account. Designing for a specific form factor or weight requirement may limit the choice of materials available. Similarly, aesthetic considerations may influence the selection of materials that can provide the desired appearance or texture.

Furthermore, cost considerations are essential in both material selection and processing. Engineers must strike a balance between performance and affordability, taking into account factors such as material availability, production volume, and market requirements.

In conclusion, designing with engineering materials requires a comprehensive understanding of the materials' properties, processing techniques, and applications. However, it is equally important to consider the design constraints that can significantly impact the final outcome. By considering factors such as mechanical requirements, environmental conditions, manufacturability, size and weight limitations, aesthetics, and cost considerations, engineers can make informed decisions and develop innovative solutions that meet the needs of their projects and the expectations of their clients.

Material Designation Systems

In the realm of materials science and engineering, understanding and correctly identifying different materials is imperative for engineers. Material designation systems play a crucial role in this process, providing a standardized way to classify and communicate the properties and characteristics of various materials. This subchapter aims to elucidate the fundamental concepts of material designation systems, their importance, and their applications in the field of engineering.

Material designation systems serve as a common language for engineers, enabling efficient communication and collaboration across different industries and disciplines. They provide a systematic approach to categorize materials based on their composition, structure, and properties. These systems typically involve alphanumeric codes, symbols, and abbreviations that represent specific materials or material families. By using designated codes, engineers can quickly identify and select the appropriate materials for their projects, ensuring optimal performance and efficiency.

One commonly used material designation system is the Unified Numbering System (UNS). Developed jointly by several international organizations, the UNS assigns a unique alphanumeric code to each material, facilitating easy identification and comparison. It covers a wide range of materials, including metals, alloys, plastics, and ceramics. The UNS code indicates the material's chemical composition, manufacturing method, and other relevant details, allowing engineers to make informed decisions regarding material selection and application.

Another prominent material designation system is the ASTM International (formerly known as the American Society for Testing and Materials) system. ASTM provides a comprehensive set of standards for various materials and their testing methods. These standards include standardized material designations that are widely adopted by engineers around the world. The ASTM designation system ensures consistency and quality in material specifications, aiding engineers in selecting materials that meet specific performance requirements.

Material designation systems are crucial in various engineering applications, such as structural design, manufacturing, and materials research. Engineers rely on these systems to identify materials with desired properties, such as strength, durability, corrosion resistance, and thermal conductivity. By utilizing the designated codes, engineers can easily compare and evaluate different materials, making informed decisions that optimize performance, cost-effectiveness, and sustainability.

In conclusion, material designation systems are indispensable tools in the field of materials science and engineering. They provide a standardized approach to classify and communicate the properties and characteristics of different materials. These systems enable efficient material selection, design, and manufacturing processes. Engineers across various industries rely on material designation systems to ensure optimal performance and reliability in their projects. By understanding and utilizing these systems, engineers can navigate the vast realm of materials knowledge, making significant advancements in technology and innovation.

Case Studies: Material Selection in Engineering Applications

In the field of engineering, selecting the right materials for various applications is a critical task that directly impacts the performance and reliability of the final product. Engineers must consider a multitude of factors, including mechanical properties, environmental conditions, cost, and manufacturability, to ensure the optimal material is chosen. In this subchapter, we will delve into several case studies highlighting the importance of material selection in engineering applications, focusing on the niche of Materials Science and Engineering.

One case study examines the selection of materials for aircraft structures. Engineers must balance the need for lightweight materials to reduce fuel consumption with the requirement for high strength and durability. By evaluating the mechanical properties, such as tensile strength and fatigue resistance, of different alloys and composites, engineers can determine the most suitable materials for specific aircraft components. The case study will highlight the importance of material testing and simulation tools in predicting the performance of these materials under extreme conditions.

Another case study explores the material selection process for medical implants. In this niche, biocompatibility and corrosion resistance are critical factors to consider. Engineers must carefully assess the compatibility of materials with the human body, ensuring they do not cause adverse reactions or lead to implant failure. The case study will delve into the use of biomaterials, such as titanium alloys and bioactive ceramics, to develop successful medical implants, taking into account the specific requirements of different applications.

A third case study focuses on material selection for renewable energy applications. As the world transitions towards sustainable energy sources, engineers face the challenge of identifying materials that are both efficient and environmentally friendly. The case study will discuss the selection of materials for solar panels, wind turbine blades, and energy storage systems. Engineers must consider factors such as thermal stability, electrical conductivity, and recyclability to ensure the longevity and sustainability of these renewable energy solutions.

Throughout this subchapter, we will emphasize the importance of a systematic approach to material selection, which involves evaluating various options, conducting experiments, and utilizing advanced simulation techniques. By showcasing real-world case studies, engineers in the field of Materials Science and Engineering will gain valuable insights into the challenges and considerations involved in material selection for different engineering applications.

In conclusion, material selection in engineering applications is a crucial process that directly influences the performance and reliability of products. By analyzing case studies across various niches, this subchapter aims to equip engineers with the knowledge and tools necessary to make informed decisions when selecting materials. Whether it is for aircraft structures, medical implants, or renewable energy systems, the right material can make all the difference in achieving efficient, sustainable, and technologically advanced solutions.

Chapter 12: Applications of Engineering Materials

Structural Materials

In the field of engineering, the study and understanding of materials play a crucial role in designing and constructing various structures. This subchapter, titled "Structural Materials," aims to provide engineers specializing in materials science and engineering with a comprehensive overview of the different types of materials used in structural applications.

Structural materials refer to those materials that are specifically chosen and engineered to withstand and support loads while preserving their integrity and stability. These materials are essential in the construction of buildings, bridges, aircraft, and many other industrial applications. The properties of structural materials are carefully considered to ensure they can endure the forces and stresses they will encounter during their service life.

This subchapter will delve into the three primary categories of structural materials: metals, polymers, and ceramics. Each category has its unique properties, advantages, and limitations, making them suitable for specific applications.

Metals, with their excellent mechanical properties, form the backbone of many structural systems. The subchapter will explore different types of metals, such as steel and aluminum, and discuss their properties, including strength, ductility, and corrosion resistance. The chapter will also cover topics like metal alloys, heat treatment, and the effect of microstructure on material properties.

Polymers, on the other hand, offer a wide range of benefits in structural applications. Their lightweight nature, corrosion resistance, and design flexibility make them ideal for certain industries. This subchapter will explore engineering polymers and composites, discussing their mechanical properties, thermal stability, and specific applications. It will also touch upon advanced manufacturing techniques, such as injection molding and 3D printing, which have revolutionized the use of polymers in structural applications.

Ceramics, known for their high-temperature resistance and hardness, find extensive use in structural materials. This subchapter will discuss different types of ceramics, such as oxides, carbides, and nitrides, and their unique properties. It will also explore their applications in aerospace, automotive, and electronic industries, including their use as coatings and cutting tools.

By the end of this subchapter, engineers specializing in materials science and engineering will have a thorough understanding of the various structural materials available, their properties, and their applications. This knowledge will enable them to make informed decisions when selecting materials for specific projects, ensuring the structural integrity and long-term durability of the structures they design and build.

Electronic and Optoelectronic Materials

In the ever-evolving field of materials science and engineering, electronic and optoelectronic materials play a crucial role in shaping the future of technology. These materials, with their unique properties and functionalities, have revolutionized the way we communicate, compute, and utilize energy. In this subchapter, we will explore the fundamentals of electronic and optoelectronic materials, their properties, processing techniques, and various applications.

Electronic materials are at the heart of modern electronic devices and systems. They possess specific electrical conductivity properties that enable the flow of electrons and are essential for the functioning of circuits and components. Some common electronic materials include semiconductors, conductors, and insulators. Semiconductors, such as silicon and gallium arsenide, exhibit a moderate level of electrical conductivity, making them ideal for applications in transistors, diodes, and integrated circuits. Conductors, such as copper and aluminum, have high electrical conductivity and are commonly used in power transmission and electrical wiring. Insulators, like rubber and glass, have very low electrical conductivity and are employed to prevent the flow of electricity.

Optoelectronic materials, on the other hand, possess properties that enable the interaction between light and electricity. They find applications in various fields, including telecommunications, photovoltaics, and displays. Optoelectronic materials can absorb, emit, or control the flow of light. One example is the light-emitting diode (LED), which is made using semiconducting materials like gallium nitride or indium phosphide. LEDs are used for lighting purposes due to their high energy efficiency and long lifespan. Another example is photovoltaic materials, like silicon, which can convert sunlight into electricity in solar cells.

The processing techniques for electronic and optoelectronic materials are diverse and depend on their specific properties. Semiconductor materials, for instance, undergo processes such as crystal growth, doping, and lithography to form intricate circuit patterns. Thin-film deposition techniques like chemical vapor deposition and sputtering are used to create functional layers in optoelectronic devices. Understanding these processing techniques is essential for engineers working in the field of materials science and engineering.

In conclusion, electronic and optoelectronic materials are critical components in the realm of materials science and engineering. Their unique properties and functionalities have paved the way for significant advancements in technology. As engineers in the field, it is essential to have a comprehensive understanding of these materials, their properties, and the processing techniques involved. With this knowledge, we can continue to push the boundaries of innovation and create a future that is driven by electronic and optoelectronic materials.

Biomaterials

In the field of materials science and engineering, biomaterials play a crucial role in developing innovative solutions for a wide range of applications in medicine and healthcare. Biomaterials are substances that interact with biological systems, either as part of a medical device, implant, or as a scaffold for tissue regeneration. They are designed to be compatible with living tissues, providing support, promoting healing, and enhancing the overall quality of life for patients.

This subchapter on biomaterials aims to provide engineers in the field of materials science and engineering with a comprehensive overview of the fundamental principles, processing techniques, and applications of biomaterials. It delves into the intricate relationship between materials and biology, highlighting the importance of understanding the biological response to different biomaterials in order to design and develop successful medical devices and implants.

The subchapter begins by introducing the basic concepts of biomaterials, including their classification based on origin (natural, synthetic, or hybrid) and their properties such as biocompatibility, bioactivity, and mechanical characteristics. It explores the challenges and considerations involved in selecting appropriate biomaterials for specific applications, taking into account factors like degradation, sterilization, and long-term performance.

Next, the subchapter covers the processing techniques used to fabricate biomaterials, including traditional methods such as casting, extrusion, and machining, as well as more advanced techniques such as electrospinning, 3D printing, and surface modification. It discusses the advantages and limitations of each method and emphasizes the importance of tailoring the processing techniques to achieve desired material properties and functionalities.

The subchapter also delves into the various applications of biomaterials, ranging from orthopedic implants and dental materials to tissue engineering and drug delivery systems. It explores the challenges faced in these applications, such as achieving optimal biocompatibility, minimizing inflammation, and ensuring long-term stability of the biomaterials.

Through this subchapter, engineers specializing in materials science and engineering will gain a solid understanding of the principles and applications of biomaterials. They will be equipped with the knowledge and tools necessary to contribute to the development of innovative biomaterials that enhance patient outcomes and improve the quality of life for individuals worldwide.

Environmental and Energy Materials

In recent years, the field of materials science and engineering has witnessed a significant shift towards the development of environmentally friendly and energy-efficient materials. This subchapter aims to provide engineers, specifically those specializing in materials science and engineering, with an overview of the various types of materials that are being developed and utilized in the pursuit of sustainable solutions.

One of the key focuses of environmental and energy materials is the reduction of carbon emissions and the mitigation of climate change. Engineers in this field are working tirelessly to develop materials that have a lower carbon footprint and can be used in a wide range of applications. For instance, lightweight and high-strength composite materials are being developed to replace conventional materials like steel and concrete, which have a high carbon content in their production processes. These new materials offer a promising solution for reducing the weight of vehicles and transportation systems, leading to improved fuel efficiency and reduced greenhouse gas emissions.

Another area of interest within environmental and energy materials is the development of energy storage systems. As the demand for renewable energy sources such as solar and wind power continues to grow, engineers are focusing on creating materials that can efficiently store and release energy. Advanced battery technologies, such as lithium-ion batteries, are being improved to increase their energy density, lifespan, and safety. Additionally, new materials for supercapacitors and hydrogen storage are being explored to enable the efficient storage and utilization of renewable energy.

Furthermore, engineers in this field are also working on materials for energy harvesting and conversion. By harnessing energy from sources such as sunlight, heat, and vibrations, these materials have the potential to power a wide range of applications, from wearable electronics to autonomous sensor networks. Materials like photovoltaics, thermoelectrics, and piezoelectrics are being researched and optimized to improve their efficiency and durability.

In summary, the field of environmental and energy materials holds great promise for engineers specializing in materials science and engineering. By developing sustainable materials with reduced carbon footprints and enhanced energy efficiency, engineers can contribute to addressing the global challenges of climate change and energy sustainability. This subchapter serves as a comprehensive introduction to the various aspects and applications of environmental and energy materials, providing engineers with the necessary knowledge to contribute to this rapidly evolving field.

Materials for Transportation

Transportation is a vital aspect of modern society, enabling the movement of people and goods across vast distances. Engineers in the field of materials science and engineering play a crucial role in developing and selecting the materials used in transportation systems. This subchapter aims to provide an overview of the various materials employed in different modes of transportation, including their properties, processing techniques, and applications.

One of the most widely used materials in transportation is steel. Its exceptional strength, toughness, and durability make it the backbone of many vehicles, such as cars, trains, and airplanes. Steel alloys with specific compositions and heat treatments can be tailored to withstand extreme conditions, such as high temperatures and corrosive environments. Furthermore, steel can be easily shaped through processes like casting, forging, and welding, making it highly versatile for various transportation applications.

Another essential material in transportation is aluminum. Its low density, coupled with excellent strength and corrosion resistance, makes it an ideal choice for aerospace and automotive industries. Aluminum alloys, such as those containing copper, magnesium, or zinc, can be used to optimize specific properties, such as strength-to-weight ratio and formability. Additionally, aluminum can be recycled easily, making it an environmentally sustainable option.

Polymeric materials, particularly composites, have gained significant attention in recent years due to their lightweight and high strength characteristics. Fiber-reinforced composites, such as carbon fiber composites, are extensively used in aerospace applications, where weight reduction is critical. These materials offer excellent strength-to-weight ratios, corrosion resistance, and fatigue performance, making them ideal for aircraft components.

For the automotive industry, polymer-based materials, including thermoplastics and thermosets, are widely employed. These materials provide excellent design flexibility, impact resistance, and corrosion resistance. Moreover, polymer composites can be tailored to specific requirements, enhancing fuel efficiency and reducing emissions.

In addition to metals and polymers, ceramics and their composites find applications in transportation, particularly for high-temperature environments. Ceramic materials possess exceptional hardness, thermal stability, and wear resistance, making them suitable for engine components and cutting tools. Ceramic matrix composites (CMCs) combine the strength of fibers with the toughness of ceramics, offering improved strength and fracture resistance.

In summary, the selection of materials for transportation systems requires careful consideration of properties, processing techniques, and applications. Steel, aluminum, polymers, and ceramics, along with their composites, each play a vital role in various modes of transportation. As engineers in the field of materials science and engineering, it is crucial to continually explore new materials and processing methods to develop innovative transportation solutions that are safe, efficient, and sustainable.

Materials for Aerospace Applications

Introduction:
Materials used in aerospace applications must possess exceptional properties to withstand the extreme conditions encountered in space and aviation. These materials must exhibit high strength, excellent resistance to corrosion and fatigue, low density, and superior thermal stability. This subchapter will explore the various materials that are extensively used in aerospace applications, including metals, alloys, composites, and ceramics.

Metals:
Metals such as aluminum, titanium, and steel alloys play a crucial role in aerospace engineering. Aluminum alloys are lightweight yet possess high strength, making them suitable for structural components. Titanium alloys offer excellent strength-to-weight ratios and resistance to corrosion, making them ideal for aircraft engine components. Steel alloys, on the other hand, provide exceptional strength and toughness, making them a popular choice for landing gears and structural supports.

Alloys:
Apart from metals, various alloy systems are used in aerospace applications. Nickel-based superalloys excel in high-temperature environments, making them ideal for turbine blades and other hot section components. Cobalt-based alloys are also used in turbine engines due to their excellent thermal stability and resistance to corrosion. Additionally, shape memory alloys find application in aerospace due to their unique ability to change shape under specific conditions.

Composites:

Composite materials, composed of two or more constituent materials, offer exceptional strength-to-weight ratios, making them highly desirable for aerospace applications. Carbon fiber-reinforced polymers (CFRP) are extensively used in aircraft structures, providing lightweight and high-strength properties. Glass fiber-reinforced polymers (GFRP) are also used in aerospace applications that require lower strength but offer better resistance to chemicals and moisture.

Ceramics:

Ceramic materials possess excellent thermal and chemical resistance, making them suitable for aerospace applications such as thermal protection systems, heat shields, and rocket nozzles. Silicon carbide and alumina are commonly used ceramics due to their high melting points and superior mechanical properties. Ceramic matrix composites (CMC) combine the advantages of ceramics and fibers, offering enhanced heat resistance and durability.

Conclusion:

Materials for aerospace applications must meet stringent requirements to withstand the extreme conditions encountered in space and aviation. Metals, alloys, composites, and ceramics all play crucial roles in aerospace engineering. Each material offers unique properties that make them suitable for specific applications. As engineers in the field of materials science and engineering, understanding the properties and applications of these materials is essential for designing and developing advanced aerospace technologies.

Chapter 13: Future Trends in Materials Science and Engineering

Emerging Materials

In the ever-evolving field of materials science and engineering, the discovery and development of new materials hold immense significance. These emerging materials present engineers with exciting opportunities to revolutionize various industries and create innovative solutions to complex challenges. This subchapter explores some of the most promising emerging materials that are transforming the landscape of engineering.

One such material is graphene, a single layer of carbon atoms arranged in a hexagonal lattice. With its exceptional electrical, mechanical, and thermal properties, graphene has the potential to revolutionize electronics, energy storage, and composite materials. Engineers are exploring its applications in flexible and transparent electronics, high-performance batteries, and even in enhancing the strength and durability of other materials.

Nanomaterials, another class of emerging materials, offer unique properties due to their extremely small size. These materials, typically measured in nanometers, exhibit enhanced strength, conductivity, and reactivity compared to their bulk counterparts. Engineers are harnessing nanomaterials for various applications, including drug delivery systems, sensors, and lightweight structural materials. The field of nanotechnology holds great promise for advancements in medicine, electronics, and environmental sustainability.

Smart materials, also known as intelligent or responsive materials, are another area of focus within the realm of emerging materials. These materials have the ability to respond to external stimuli, such as temperature, light, or pressure, by changing their physical properties. Shape memory alloys, for example, can return to their original shape when heated, making them ideal for applications such as self-repairing structures and medical devices. Engineers are exploring the potential of smart materials in diverse fields including aerospace, robotics, and healthcare.

Biocompatible materials are also gaining significant attention in engineering. These materials are designed to interact harmoniously with living tissues, making them invaluable for medical implants, drug delivery systems, and tissue engineering. The development of biocompatible materials has opened up new possibilities for personalized medicine, regenerative therapies, and prosthetics, ultimately improving the quality of life for patients.

In conclusion, the exploration of emerging materials is an exciting frontier for engineers in the field of materials science and engineering. Graphene, nanomaterials, smart materials, and biocompatible materials are just a few examples of the many groundbreaking materials that are reshaping the future of engineering. By harnessing the unique properties of these materials, engineers can innovate and create solutions that were once deemed unimaginable. As the field of materials science continues to advance, engineers must stay at the forefront of these emerging materials to unlock their full potential and drive the next wave of technological advancements.

Nanomaterials and Nanotechnology

Nanomaterials and nanotechnology have revolutionized the field of materials science and engineering. As engineers, it is crucial to understand the principles, properties, and applications of these remarkable materials, as they offer unprecedented opportunities for innovation and advancement in various industries.

Nanomaterials are substances that possess unique properties due to their nanoscale dimensions, typically ranging from 1 to 100 nanometers. At this scale, materials exhibit novel mechanical, electrical, thermal, and optical characteristics, which differ significantly from their bulk counterparts. This enables engineers to design and create materials with enhanced performance and functionalities.

Nanotechnology, on the other hand, encompasses the manipulation and control of matter at the nanoscale to develop new materials, devices, and systems. It involves the synthesis, characterization, and application of nanomaterials in various fields, such as electronics, energy, medicine, and environmental science.

One of the most significant advantages of nanomaterials is their large surface area-to-volume ratio. This property allows for improved reactivity, making them ideal for catalysis and sensing applications. Additionally, their unique optical properties enable the development of advanced sensors, solar cells, and displays. For engineers in the field of electronics, nanomaterials offer the potential for smaller, faster, and more efficient devices.

Nanomaterials also possess remarkable mechanical properties. Their high strength and toughness make them suitable for structural applications, such as lightweight composites and coatings. Furthermore, their flexibility and elasticity are advantageous for applications in wearable electronics and biomedical devices.

In the field of healthcare, nanomaterials have revolutionized drug delivery systems, imaging techniques, and tissue engineering. By engineering nanoparticles with specific surface functionalities, drugs can be targeted to specific cells or tissues, improving efficacy and reducing side effects. Nanomaterials also enable highly sensitive diagnostic imaging, allowing for early disease detection.

As engineers, it is essential to understand the challenges associated with working with nanomaterials, such as potential toxicity and environmental impact. Therefore, responsible and ethical design and manufacturing practices must be implemented to ensure the safe and sustainable use of nanotechnology.

In conclusion, nanomaterials and nanotechnology have revolutionized the field of materials science and engineering. Their unique properties and vast array of applications offer endless possibilities for innovation. As engineers in the field, understanding the principles, properties, and applications of nanomaterials is essential for pushing the boundaries of technology and driving advancements in various industries.

Sustainable Materials

Sustainable Materials: Paving the Way for a Greener Future

In recent years, the field of materials science and engineering has witnessed a significant shift towards sustainable practices. As engineers, it is crucial for us to understand the importance of sustainable materials and their potential to revolutionize various industries. This subchapter aims to provide an overview of sustainable materials and their applications, enabling engineers to make informed decisions and contribute to a greener future.

Sustainable materials, also known as eco-friendly or green materials, are those that are responsibly sourced, produced, used, and disposed of, with minimal impact on the environment and human health. These materials are designed to address the challenges of resource depletion, pollution, and climate change. They offer numerous advantages, including reduced energy consumption, lower greenhouse gas emissions, and improved recyclability.

One key aspect of sustainable materials is their renewable nature. Renewable materials are derived from natural sources that can be replenished over time, such as bamboo, cork, and hemp. Not only do these materials have a significantly lower environmental footprint than traditional alternatives, but they also possess unique properties that make them suitable for various applications. For instance, bamboo is lightweight, durable, and has excellent tensile strength, making it an ideal substitute for wood in construction.

Another category of sustainable materials is recycled materials. These materials are produced by reprocessing waste products, diverting them from landfills and reducing the need for virgin resources. Examples of recycled materials include recycled plastics, glass, and paper. Using recycled materials in engineering applications can significantly decrease the demand for raw materials, conserve energy, and reduce the release of harmful pollutants during production.

In addition to renewable and recycled materials, sustainable engineering also involves the development of biodegradable materials. These materials have the ability to break down naturally over time, reducing their impact on the environment. Biodegradable polymers, for instance, can replace conventional plastics in applications such as packaging and biomedical devices. By choosing biodegradable materials, engineers can contribute to the reduction of plastic waste and the preservation of ecosystems.

Furthermore, sustainable materials are not limited to the realm of natural resources. Advances in nanotechnology have led to the development of innovative materials with enhanced properties and sustainability features. For example, nanocomposites can improve the mechanical strength and durability of materials while reducing their weight and environmental impact.

As engineers, it is our responsibility to prioritize sustainable materials in our designs and processes. By incorporating these materials into our projects, we can minimize the environmental impact of our work and contribute to a more sustainable future. This subchapter serves as a starting point for understanding sustainable materials and their applications, empowering engineers to make informed decisions that benefit both our profession and the planet.

Materials for 3D Printing

In recent years, 3D printing has revolutionized the field of engineering by allowing engineers to create complex and customized objects with ease. This technology has opened up new avenues for innovation and has significantly impacted various industries, from aerospace to healthcare. One of the key factors that determine the success of a 3D printing project is the choice of materials. In this subchapter, we will explore the various materials commonly used in 3D printing and their properties.

1. Polymers: Polymers are the most widely used materials in 3D printing due to their versatility and affordability. They can be easily melted and extruded layer by layer to create intricate designs. Some commonly used polymers include acrylonitrile butadiene styrene (ABS), polylactic acid (PLA), and polyamide (PA). These polymers offer different mechanical properties, such as strength, flexibility, and heat resistance, making them suitable for various applications.

2. Metals: Metal 3D printing has gained popularity in industries where high strength and durability are required. Materials like stainless steel, titanium, and aluminum can be used to create strong and lightweight components. Metal powders are sintered or melted using laser or electron beam technology to build up the desired object layer by layer. Metal 3D printing has immense potential in aerospace, automotive, and medical industries.

3. Ceramics: Ceramics offer excellent thermal and electrical properties, making them suitable for applications where high temperature resistance is required. They can be used to create intricate designs with

fine details. Ceramic materials like alumina, zirconia, and silicon nitride are commonly used in 3D printing. Ceramic 3D printing finds applications in electronics, aerospace, and medical industries.

4. Composites: Composites are materials made by combining two or more different materials to achieve enhanced properties. In 3D printing, composites are used to create objects with improved strength, stiffness, and other desired characteristics. Carbon fiber reinforced polymers (CFRPs) and glass fiber reinforced polymers (GFRPs) are commonly used composites in 3D printing.

5. Biomaterials: 3D printing has also found applications in the field of medicine and healthcare. Biomaterials, such as biocompatible polymers and hydrogels, are used to create customized implants, prosthetics, and tissue scaffolds. These materials have the ability to mimic the properties of natural tissues and organs, enabling the development of patient-specific medical solutions.

In conclusion, the choice of materials for 3D printing plays a crucial role in determining the success of a project. Engineers must carefully consider the requirements of their application and select materials that offer the desired mechanical, thermal, and electrical properties. The continuous development of new materials for 3D printing is expanding the possibilities for engineers in the fields of materials science and engineering, driving innovation and pushing the boundaries of what can be achieved through this transformative technology.

Materials for Advanced Electronics

In the ever-evolving field of electronics, advancements are constantly being made to create faster, smaller, and more efficient devices. These innovations would not be possible without the development of advanced materials that possess unique properties and characteristics. This subchapter explores the fascinating world of materials for advanced electronics, delving into their properties, processing methods, and applications.

One of the key materials that revolutionized the electronics industry is silicon. Its exceptional properties, such as high thermal conductivity, excellent electrical insulation, and easily modifiable properties, have made it the backbone of modern electronic devices. However, as the demand for higher performance and miniaturization continues to grow, engineers are turning to alternative materials to overcome the limitations of silicon.

One such material is graphene, a single layer of carbon atoms arranged in a hexagonal lattice. Graphene possesses extraordinary electrical conductivity, thermal conductivity, and mechanical strength, making it an ideal candidate for various electronic applications. Its two-dimensional nature also enables the creation of flexible and transparent electronics, paving the way for futuristic devices.

Another advanced material gaining attention in the electronics industry is gallium nitride (GaN). GaN offers superior power handling capabilities, high electron mobility, and excellent thermal conductivity. These properties make it suitable for power electronics, light-emitting diodes (LEDs), and radio frequency (RF) devices. GaN-based power devices have the potential to significantly improve energy efficiency and reduce the size of power converters, leading to smaller and more energy-efficient electronic systems.

In addition to graphene and GaN, this subchapter explores other emerging materials such as organic semiconductors, perovskites, and 2D transition metal dichalcogenides. These materials exhibit unique electrical, optical, and mechanical properties that can be harnessed for various electronic applications, including flexible displays, solar cells, and sensors.

Furthermore, the subchapter discusses the processing methods employed to fabricate these materials into functional electronic devices. Techniques such as molecular beam epitaxy, chemical vapor deposition, and printing technologies are explored, highlighting their advantages and limitations.

As engineers in the field of materials science and engineering, understanding the properties and applications of advanced materials for electronics is crucial. This subchapter equips engineers with the knowledge necessary to stay at the forefront of the rapidly advancing electronics industry, enabling them to develop innovative solutions and contribute to the future of electronics.

Chapter 14: Conclusion and Summary

Recap of Key Concepts

In this subchapter, we will provide a comprehensive recap of the key concepts covered in the book "Engineering Materials: Properties, Processing, and Applications" for engineers in the field of Materials Science and Engineering.

One of the fundamental concepts discussed throughout the book is the structure of materials. Engineers in this field must have a solid understanding of the atomic and crystal structures of different materials, as these structures greatly influence the material's properties and behavior. The subchapter will revisit the different types of crystal structures, such as cubic, hexagonal, and tetragonal, and the impact they have on mechanical, thermal, and electrical properties.

Another crucial concept covered in the book is the relationship between processing techniques and material properties. Engineers must be aware of the various manufacturing processes used to shape, join, and modify materials. These processes include casting, forming, machining, and heat treatment, among others. The subchapter will recap the advantages and limitations of each process, helping engineers make informed decisions when selecting the most suitable technique for a given application.

Understanding the mechanical properties of materials is also essential for engineers. This includes concepts such as stress, strain, elasticity, plasticity, and fracture mechanics. The subchapter will summarize these concepts, highlighting their significance in designing materials that can withstand different loads and stresses.

Furthermore, the book emphasizes the importance of material selection for specific applications. Engineers must consider factors such as mechanical, thermal, electrical, and corrosion properties when choosing materials. The subchapter will provide a concise recap of the key considerations for material selection, enabling engineers to make informed decisions based on the desired application requirements.

Lastly, the subchapter will review the importance of materials testing and characterization. Engineers need to be familiar with various testing techniques to evaluate the quality and performance of materials. This includes mechanical testing, thermal analysis, microscopy, and spectroscopy. The recap will provide a brief overview of these techniques, reminding engineers of their significance in assessing the properties and behavior of materials.

In conclusion, the subchapter "Recap of Key Concepts" serves as a valuable refresher for engineers in the field of Materials Science and Engineering. By revisiting important concepts such as material structures, processing techniques, mechanical properties, material selection, and testing, engineers can enhance their understanding and make informed decisions when working with engineering materials.

Future Prospects in Materials Science and Engineering

As engineers in the field of Materials Science and Engineering, it is crucial to stay updated with the latest advancements and future prospects in our field. The ever-evolving nature of this discipline presents us with exciting opportunities and challenges that will shape the world in the coming years.

One of the key areas with immense potential for growth is the development of advanced materials. With the increasing demand for materials with superior properties and functionalities, researchers are exploring new materials that can revolutionize various industries. For instance, the emergence of nanotechnology has opened up possibilities for the creation of materials with unique properties at the nanoscale. These nanomaterials have the potential to enhance the performance of electronics, energy storage systems, and even healthcare devices.

Furthermore, the field of biomaterials has gained significant attention due to its potential to improve medical treatments and procedures. Engineers are now focusing on developing biocompatible materials that can seamlessly integrate with the human body and aid in tissue regeneration, drug delivery, and even the development of artificial organs. These advancements hold the promise of transforming healthcare and improving the quality of life for millions of people.

Another area of interest is sustainable materials and green engineering. As the world becomes more environmentally conscious, there is a growing need for materials that are eco-friendly, energy-efficient, and recyclable. Engineers are now working towards developing materials that have a minimal environmental impact throughout their lifecycle. This includes the use of renewable resources, designing materials for easy recycling, and reducing energy consumption during manufacturing processes. The future of Materials Science and Engineering lies in the development of sustainable materials that can help combat climate change and preserve our planet.

Moreover, the integration of materials with emerging technologies such as artificial intelligence (AI) and Internet of Things (IoT) presents a promising avenue for innovation. These technologies can enhance the functionality and performance of materials by enabling real-time monitoring, self-healing capabilities, and adaptive behavior. For example, smart materials can respond to external stimuli and change their properties accordingly, making them ideal for applications in aerospace, automotive, and robotics industries.

In conclusion, the future prospects in Materials Science and Engineering are vast and exciting. With advancements in nanotechnology, biomaterials, sustainable materials, and the integration of emerging technologies, engineers in this field have the opportunity to revolutionize industries and contribute to a sustainable and technologically advanced future. It is essential for us as engineers to stay abreast of these developments, embrace innovation, and continue pushing the boundaries of what is possible in Materials Science and Engineering.

Final Thoughts

As we conclude this comprehensive journey through the world of engineering materials, it is important for engineers in the field of materials science and engineering to reflect upon the key concepts and insights gained. Throughout this book, we have explored the fundamental properties, various processing techniques, and practical applications of engineering materials, with the ultimate goal of enhancing our understanding and ability to create innovative solutions.

One of the key takeaways from this exploration is the crucial role that materials play in the success of any engineering project. As engineers, we must not only possess a deep understanding of the properties and behaviors of different materials, but also be able to select the most suitable ones for each specific application. This requires a careful balance of technical knowledge, creativity, and problem-solving skills.

Furthermore, the importance of materials processing techniques cannot be overstated. The way in which materials are shaped, treated, and assembled significantly impacts their performance and functionality. From traditional methods such as casting and forging to cutting-edge techniques like additive manufacturing, we have covered a wide range of processing techniques that enable engineers to optimize the properties of materials for their intended use.

In addition to understanding the properties and processing of materials, engineers must also stay up-to-date with the latest advancements and emerging trends in the field. Materials science and engineering is a rapidly evolving discipline, with new materials being discovered and developed regularly. By keeping a finger on the pulse of innovation, engineers can leverage these advancements to push the boundaries of what is possible and create groundbreaking solutions.

Finally, it is important to emphasize the significance of collaboration and interdisciplinary approaches in materials science and engineering. The challenges we face in developing new materials and applications are often complex and multifaceted. By working together with experts from various fields, such as chemistry, physics, and mechanical engineering, we can combine our knowledge and expertise to tackle these challenges more effectively and unlock new opportunities.

In conclusion, the study of engineering materials is a continuous journey that requires a lifelong commitment to learning, innovation, and collaboration. By mastering the properties, processing techniques, and applications of materials, engineers in the field of materials science and engineering can make significant contributions to society and shape the future of technology. Let this book be your guide as you embark on this exciting and rewarding path.

www.ingramcontent.com/pod-product-compliance
Lightning Source LLC
LaVergne TN
LVHW021828060526
838201LV00058B/3551